FOOTLOOSE

SYDNEY TO LONDON

MARK WALTERS

CONTENTS

The prices mentioned throughout this book have been converted from the local currency into British Pounds (£) using the exchange rates in the respective countries at the time I was in them.

AUSTRALIA

SYDNEY

A famous Chinese man - not famous enough for me to know his name - once said, "The journey of a thousand miles begins with a single step." My first step - and don't worry, I won't write about every one of them - is towards customs at Sydney's Kingsford Smith Airport. Due to carrying one hundred ultra-strength anti-histamine pills with me, I'm concerned about walking through. These are prescription-only drugs in Australia, and I don't have a prescription for them.

The customs card asks: "Are you bringing into Australia goods that may be prohibited or subject to restrictions, such as medicines, steroids, illegal pornography, firearms, weapons, or illicit drugs?" I've ticked "Yes". It's odd that they've lumped medicines in with items like firearms and illegal pornography. There should be individual boxes to tick, so you can be specific about the contraband you're bringing in. Ticking that catch-all box on the customs card, along with the red flags of not having an onward flight ticket, not having any accommodation booked, and not having a job back home to return to, leaves me fearing I may be getting an overly personal, backside-focused welcome to Australia.

The guy checking the cards does a double-take when he looks at mine, then sends me to lane nine in the customs area. Lanes one, two, and three are busy with families, back-packers, and businessmen; four to eight aren't in use; nine is empty apart from two uniformed officials - a man built like a rugby player and a woman with a face like one. They look me up and down and then wave me through without even looking inside my bag. I'm pleased about this - it allows my dignity to remain intact - but also miffed that they took one look at me and decided I wasn't capable of being a badass, gun-wielding, cocaine smuggler. On the flip side, I guess I should take it as a compliment that they took one look at me and decided I wasn't the sort of person who packs a DVD of *Return Of The Donkey Dong*. I wish I hadn't binned my copy before coming here.

I check into a £22 a night hostel near Sydney Central Station. I've never stayed in a hostel before because I don't find urine-stained bunks riddled with bed bugs - snorers to the left of me, masturbators to the right - to be conducive to a good night's sleep. But the sky-high hotel prices in Australia give me no option. I tell one of my roommates about my plan to travel from here to London without flying, and that I've packed little for the trip - 10 kg in total. "You haven't got a towel? Or trainers? Or shorts?" he says.

"Hahaha. That's tickled me that has. I'll be looking out for you on the news. I can see the headlines now: 'British tourist with only a toothbrush found dead in the Outback'."

For footwear, I have only plain, black, rubber flip-flops. I believe flip-flops are the pinnacle of the footwear tree. They're inexpensive, comfortable, convenient, hard-wearing, and waterproof - and you don't have to waste money and bag space on socks. At this point, you may doubt the superiority of flip-flops over other types of footwear. But in the time it takes you to finish reading this book you'll see the error of your ways. You'll realise what a fool you've been for spending your life to date wearing trainers and shoes.

After unpacking, I catch a bus to Bondi Beach, 8 km from the city centre. A kilometre of golden sand stretches along the foaming swells of the South Pacific Ocean. Denim-shorted girls in oversized sunglasses lick ice creams and sip fresh-pressed juices; shaggy-haired, shirtless dudes flip tricks on BMXs and skateboards; Lycra-clad exercisers pound along the promenade; and toned, bronzed bodies lounge on the sand. Untoned, ghostly bodies too.

It's only on a beach that you get to see all the shapes and sizes that people come in. On a beach, with clothes shed and free of make-up and hair gel, you realise everyone has a flaw or two - or, in some cases, ten - that those carefully chosen filtered Facebook photos don't show. Something about being on a beach makes people just not care. Those guys and girls who usually spend ages getting ready every morning throw caution to the wind when on a beach. Their love-handles are on show, their hair looks like a scarecrow's, and they have sand coming out their nostrils. And that's ok because people don't judge each other on a beach. It's a judgment ceasefire. The only ones who are fair game for stares and whispers are those who turn up in jeans and without a towel.

Bondi Beach being the Mecca of the surf world, it's no surprise to see a hundred-plus surfers in the sea. Some pull off cool moves; others - tourists who have underestimated how hard surfing is - spend the afternoon being tossed around and half-drowned. I wait about hoping to see a shark attack. Anything between a mauling and a lick would be okay. No deaths need to occur for my amusement. I ask one of the lifeguards if they get many sharks here.

"Yeah, mate," he says. "We've had a few great whites here in the last month. Two of them got caught in the shark net half a kilometre out. The other one, some of the guys got on jet skis to scare it off."

The job of a lifeguard on Bondi Beach is in many ways ideal: sitting in the sun on one of the world's premier beaches, eating Cornettos while bikini-clad women throw themselves at you. But having to get on a jet ski now and then to play chicken with a killer shark takes the shine off of it; to the extent I've changed my mind about asking for an application form.

Back in the city centre, I visit Hyde Park Barracks, which housed convicts sent to Sydney from the UK in the 1800s. Records on the walls show the British sent most here for minor crimes. One says that Patrick Conaghan, a twenty-five-year-old sailor, received a sentence of seven years in Australia for stealing a cow. How times have changed. Someone in the UK arrested for stealing a cow these days would get a caution and be let go the same day. That's if the police even took the incident seriously. If someone called 999 and said, "Daisy's been taken. She's black and white and has a lovely set of udders," he'd be told to stop taking the piss. Convicts sent to Sydney were kept here rather than in prison because no one had gotten around to building one. Pubs, bookies, and brothels were higher on the list of construction priorities. Their sentence was primarily work-based, and it was their slogging that kick-started Sydney into becoming a great city.

After Hyde Park, I head to the city's most famous building, the Sydney Opera House, which juts into the glittering water of Darling Harbour. There's no denying its white, curved, multi-peaked roof - designed to mimic the sails of the thousands of vessels that pass it each day - makes for an iconic monument. From a distance, anyway. Up close, it looks faded and dated. With its dirty tiles, bare concrete underside, and brown and yellow pebbledash floor and walls, it looks like a council swimming pool complex built in the seventies. It was only supposed to cost £4,000,000, but they overspent by a whopping £52,000,000. For that price, I'd expect not only a swimming pool but a full-size aquarium with the world's largest whale in it.

The Rocks area of Sydney's harbour was for a century known as the rough part of the city. A pub here, The Hero of Waterloo, used to be infamous for plying men with free drinks until they passed out, at which point they'd be dropped through a trapdoor into the cellar, then dragged through a secret tunnel that ran to the docks, where they were sold to the navy. When they woke, they would be out at sea, with no choice but to get on with their new life. The pub claims not to do the get-you-pissed-then-sell-you-to-the-navy trick anymore, but I decide not to have a drink there - free or not - just in case.

Now rejuvenated and gentrified, The Rocks is a trendy area with shady trees and outdoor terraces. It's also the entry point for crossing the Sydney Harbour Bridge - the world's largest steel arch bridge, which looks like a huge coat hanger. It's not a good idea to hang stuff off it, though. Engineers are worried the extra weight from the hundreds of layers of lead paint added to it over its eighty-year history have affected its structural properties and could cause it to collapse. Some poor sods now have to scrape those layers of paint off. Probably gap year students getting £1 for each kilogram of paint they remove. Those guys will do anything for beer money: picking grapes, licking stamps, giving blowjobs, etc.

Back at the dorm room, there's a spotty, spectacled lad stood over two open suitcases filled mostly with Lego, but also other assorted toys, like cars and action figures. He spots me staring and says, "I know, I'm crazy. But it's my Lego collection, and I need it. I'm moving to the US to live with my girlfriend, and there's no way I'm leaving it behind."

You can make anything from Lego these days - even bombs. He should be more worried about going through customs in America than I was about going through customs here. He'll get locked up by a shouty man with a crew cut: "We know your sort, coming over here and hating on our baseball, McDonald's, and homosexuals. You're planning to blow up our liberal asses with a Lego bomb. We know it, boy, and we're going to get you to say it. Sergeant Johnson, get the torture room ready. Err, I mean the enhanced interrogation room."

MELBOURNE

I arrived in Melbourne yesterday evening after an eleven-hour train ride from Sydney. There are long-standing arguments over which of the two is Australia's premier city. Neither, though, is the capital; Canberra was chosen because it's an equal distance between the two, and to prevent whoever didn't get picked starting a civil war. Choosing Canberra was the wrong decision. It's like having a couple of charismatic stunners begging for it and, not being able to decide between the two, instead opting for a boring minger.

Today, exploring the city, I see the iconic row of clocks above the steps to Flinders Street train station (Australia's oldest one); get purposely lost around the hipster-heaving, Victorian-era laneways; and walk along Batman Avenue to the Melbourne Cricket Ground. Batman Avenue is named after an explorer called John Batman, not Batman the super-hero. But if you include Batman in the name of anything, regardless of your intention, you've effectively named it after the caped crusader, as that's what everyone will assume.

With a capacity of one-hundred thousand, the Melbourne Cricket Ground is the largest cricket stadium in the world. It was the venue, in 1877, for the first cricket match between Australia and England, of which there have been hundreds since. The sporting rivalry between the two countries is intense. They hate us; we hate them. Hate isn't fashionable these days, with everyone jumping on the love-and-hugs bandwagon, but is okay so long as there's an equal amount on both sides and no weapons are used. The rivalry isn't one in which the English - or the whinging poms, as the Aussies refer to us - do well. Australia regularly smashes us at cricket and rugby. But if you factor in snooker and darts - sports for fat, lazy people, which the English are better at than most - the Convicts vs Poms score card evens out. The next match in the Ashes, a bi-annual series of cricket matches between the two countries, which both consider as important as the Cricket World Cup, takes place at this stadium in a few days time. I won't be staying around for it unless they let me play. Given the situation - three down in a best of five series - they may as well.

Afterwards, I go to the train station to book tickets from Melbourne to Adelaide, and from Adelaide to Alice Springs. I plan to take trains up to the north coast of Australia, then get on a boat of some sort - like a yacht, if I can blag my way onto one - heading to somewhere in Asia. But the clerk at the station tells me trains on those routes - which are primarily for freight trains, not passenger ones - only run twice a month, and it being the Christmas period they're not running at all. This means several nine-hour-plus bus jour-neys instead. I hate buses. They're a shite way to travel. They take ages, and you're in with the worst of society. It's the mode of transport favoured by drunks, paupers, and - worst of all - backpackers. I'm a backpacker, and I wouldn't want to sit next to me on a bus.

On a tram back to the hostel, a young woman stands and

offers her seat to another woman, which she accepts. The woman now sitting says, loudly and meant for another seated guy and me to hear, "It's always the women who give up their seat these days; never the men."

I always offer my seat to someone who needs it more than me, but this woman, at forty-ish, isn't old, and there's nothing wrong with her - not physically, anyway. I leave it too long to come back with a witty retort, but decide I can't leave it like that. When we reach my stop, I stand and walk off the tram, dragging my left leg slightly behind me at an odd angle. The look on the seated woman's face is priceless. Pretending to be disabled to get one over on someone isn't something Jesus, Gandhi, or Mandela would have done - or at least admitted to having done. I'm not proud of doing it, but it's a useful tactic to be able to call upon. Don't knock it until you've tried it. That said, don't be a twat by using it to park in disabled parking spaces. That's inexcusable - unless you have a hangover.

In the afternoon, with the guys from my dorm room, I go to a barbecue-style Christmas party taking place on the rooftop terrace of the hostel. We take a crate of beers with us, which cost £27 from an off-licence. Alcohol is more expensive in Australia than in any country I've been to before. Cigarettes too, at an eye-watering £12 a pack. Chocolate has also been taxed to the max. A bar costs about £1.50 - twice as much as in the UK. That's the way to stop people eating unhealthy food: whack up the price of it. If a multipack of Toblerones cost £27, our obese friends would think twice before devouring the whole lot in one sitting.

After the rooftop event, I join a bar crawl being run by

the hostel. Twenty or so of us head out in Santa hats to sample the delights of Melbourne's nightlife. Even though I'm with a pack of Santas who are singing Christmas carols, it doesn't feel Christmassy. The locals have done their best by putting up trees and decorations, but it's too warm and too light. People are wandering around in sunglasses and shorts, not scarves and coats. It feels false and futile, like a school disco trying to pull off an Ibiza club night vibe by stringing up some fairy lights in the sports hall and playing a Pete Tong CD on a ghetto blaster.

The night gets cut short at 10 pm when five of the group, myself included, are denied entry to the club: me for wearing flip-flops, and four other guys for being "too old", despite only being in their forties. If I'd known Melbournians consider that to be old, I'd have given up my seat on the tram. Walking back to the hostel with the old-timers, I resolve to start a campaign to tackle flip-flop discrimination. I have a dream that our children will one day live in a world where they will not be judged by the style of their footwear, but by the content of their character. I have a dream that one day, down in Melbourne, flip-flopped boys and flip-flopped girls will be able to join hands with shoed boys and shoed girls as sisters and brothers, and party in harmony, as one. I have a dream.

COOBER PEDY

I spent the last couple of days in Adelaide, a pretty crappy place. The highlight was seeing what claims to be the world's largest rocking horse. It is indeed big, but it doesn't look like a horse, and it no longer rocks. They've retained the title based only on the absence of competition.

Now, I'm on a bus to Coober Pedy, a destination chosen solely on the basis that it's about halfway between Adelaide and Alice Springs on my mission northwards to Darwin. The journey of eleven hours is almost entirely along a single road - the Stuart Highway - which stretches all the way up to the northern coast.

On the way, we pass Anna Creek Station, the world's largest cattle ranch. At 24,000 km², it's bigger than Israel. Maybe we can move the Israelis here. The twenty thousand cows living on the ranch wouldn't be happy but would throw fewer stones than the Palestinians.

Now and then, as we cross the bleak expanse of nothingness known as the Outback, the bus pulls over by padlocked metal boxes on the roadside, and the driver gets out to either take parcels out or put them in. Either officially or unofficially, the bus driver is doubling-up as a postman. At one such stop, he disembarks and disappears down a driveway towards an unlit, wooden building. After ten minutes, he's still not back, and we're sat on the bus, in the dark, in the middle of nowhere, wondering what's happening. It feels like a scene from a horror movie. I imagine people one by one getting off the bus to investigate, and then hearing screams as blood splatters against the bus windows and disembodied heads roll out of bushes.

Once we're on the move again - with all heads still attached to bodies - I contemplate being on a bus with people I don't know, heading to a town I don't know, at a time when most people are going home to spend Christmas with loved ones. Few are willing to be away from home at Christmas, seeing it as a sacred event that can't be missed. It's not that special, though; it happens every year, and it's mostly the same every year. If you miss one or two, or even half a dozen, it's no big deal. You've experienced many before, and there are more to come - unless Al-Qaeda captures Santa during his Middle East deliveries. It's actually good to miss a few Christmases. The ones you skip give you a greater appreciation for those that come in the future. It brings the freshness back, which gets lost after going through the same palaver year on year without a break.

As for the rest of the year, in any given month, there might be, say, twenty-five hours of quality family and friends time you miss out on if travelling long-term. There are about five hundred waking hours per month, so the good stuff missed equates to only 5% of the time. The other 95% is worth missing. And when you see the same people week after week, meet-ups merge and blur, and most of what's said and done gets forgotten. Whereas when you see people less, you're more involved and more focused when you do see them. The moments being fewer become more valuable, more memorable.

At another stop, this time at a gas station, I get off the bus to stretch my legs. A rough-looking bloke wearing cargo shorts and a dirty, white t-shirt, who I saw putting a metal case in the hold at the bus station in Adelaide, starts talking to me. His eyes light up when I tell him I'm going to Coober Pedy. He says he lives there and insists I stay at his place. I tell him I'll think about it, but think to myself that there's no chance I will. With horror movies still on my mind, I fear going to a small town in the Outback and staying with a stranger met on a bus is a scenario that will conclude with me getting an axe to the head and being tossed down a mine.

The sun has yet to rise when the bus pulls into Coober Pedy, and the place is dead. Ash, the guy I spoke with at the gas station, is still insisting I stay with him. His wife turns up in a battered pick-up truck. He opens the truck door for me. "Come on, mate," he says. "It's Christmas Eve. What the heck else are you going to do?!"

It's a good point. My options are limited. And he wouldn't kill me at Christmas, would he? He's less likely to, anyway.

Their home is a shack-like bungalow with three bedrooms - two used to store junk and tools. There's a bare concrete floor throughout. Out the back is a small, sandy yard, in which stands the rusted frame of a pig stable that adjoins a barn filled with more junk and tools. A dozen chickens and a rooster roam. When Ash starts chasing the chickens, the rooster attacks him, trying to claw him. Ash's Labrador intervenes, barking and snapping. The rooster attacks the dog too. When the rooster pauses for a second, Ash grabs it and throws it onto the roof of the bungalow.

Ash takes me on a tour of the town, a dreary place in a desolate setting: a red, rocky desert decorated with abandoned machinery and mounds of dug-up dirt. A couple of decades ago, he tells me, the town was booming on the back of opal mining, but as opal finds dried up, and the price of the stone tanked, few had reason to stay. I'm introduced to some of those who did. Mick lives in a self-built house in a cave and pines for the pre-9/11 days when you could buy dynamite without a licence. Debs runs a subterranean hotel that was once a mine and has an extensive collection of opals - some priced at £10,000+ - that she can't sell. Tony lives in "the bush" and wears threadbare boots that don't match.

Ash invites Tony to his house, and we sit drinking XXXX in the backyard on upturned milk crates. Tony is prone to random tangents, like a fifteen minute one about the Pyramids being built by Martians. When I ask why he lives outdoors, he says, "It's better living out there; there's less to worry about. When it's dark, I go to bed; when it's light, I wake up; when I'm hungry, I eat. I don't have a watch or calendar. I didn't even know it was Christmas until Ash told me."

I ask what he does for food. "There's loads out there," he says, "if you know your way about the land. I shoot emus, rabbits, and kangaroos. An average-sized kangaroo lasts me a week."

Ash and Tony, who sometimes go out together with pick-axes to look for opal, discuss places to go digging. I ask how they know where to look for it. "The truth is," says Ash, "it's complete luck. You may as well take your hat off, close your eyes and spin around, and throw the hat as far as you can. Wherever it lands is as good a place to dig as any other. I've got mates who swear by certain strategies, but every one of them has a shit heap of a car, so I call bullshit on their strategies."

Later, Tony says he's going for a walk. He comes back after two hours, which Ash says is quick for Tony: "Last time he said he was going for a walk, no one saw him again for nine months."

In the evening, Ash and Ayde, his wife, cook a tasty dinner, which we tuck into with Tony. Afterwards, we sit for hours drinking beers and playing cards.

I was a stranger on a bus to Ash, but he took me in, made me feel welcome, and - best of all - got me pissed. I've been made to feel like a long-time friend; a family member, even.

I'll still be sleeping with one eye open, though. In the yard, I saw an axe.

DARWIN

I at last reach Darwin, on Australia's northern coast. It's taken fifty-plus hours on buses to get from Sydney to here. The next leg of the trip, to Asia, will need to be by boat because buses sink in water.

My plan is to buy an eyepatch and a copy of *Moby Dick* and hang around the harbour singing shanties until a ship bound for East Timor or Indonesia, the two nearest Asian countries to Darwin, lets me aboard. But the receptionist at the hostel says I'd be better off shaving, wearing a nice shirt, and going to the Darwin Sailing Club, so I do that instead. I ask the barman there about boats heading to Asia.

"Not at this time of year," he says. "You've timed it wrong. Darwin has a tropical climate, similar to that of Southeast Asian countries. It's sunny for most of the year, but now it's the start of the stormy season. Come back in

June, when there are rallies and races going on. Loads of yachts go to Asia at that time. I'm sure someone will take you."

Heading back to the hostel, I get chatting to Terry, a sixty-something-year-old with a flannel on his head, stood drinking beer beside a camper van. "Dinah Beach Cruising Yacht Association is your best shot," he tells me. "That's where the lower class yachties hang out. I used to be a regular there, but they barred me for getting pissed and starting fights."

A thirty-minute walk later, I arrive at the Dinah Beach Cruising Yacht Association. The woman at the bar points to a couple of bearded sailor-types sat at a table in the corner and says they're the ones to ask. I go over to them.

Me: "Do you know anyone who's sailing to Asia soon?"

Sailor One: "Ha! Do you hear that?! The pom wants to go to Asia!"

Sailor Two: "You'd be unlucky if you did find someone to take you. They'd be taking you to your death. It's the cyclone season."

Sailor One: "Even if you avoid one of those, a minute of bad weather can flip over a boat."

Sailor Two: "We know everyone here and they'll all say no, but if you've got a death wish you could try your luck at Tipperary Waters Marina down the road."

I thank them for their advice and walk to Tipperary Waters Marina.

Yachts are moored at the marina, but its bars and shops are closed. The noticeboard is bare except for a few adverts offering boats for sale. If I call my bank to ask for £15,000 to buy a boat so I can sail to Asia, they'll tell him me to sod off, and also ask when I'm paying back what I already owe them.

I'm about to leave when I spot a man exiting a yacht to go to his car. "You won't find anyone to take you at this time of year," he tells me. "Not going to happen. No chance. No way. You could buy a rubber dinghy and have a go yourself, or you can fly. It's only £100 to fly to Bali from Darwin."

———

At thirty-six degrees, yesterday was the highest January temperature in Darwin since records began. This morning, though, it's raining non-stop, and there's a brooding menace in the grey sky. And the news issued a warning: a cyclone currently off the north-west coast of Australia may hit Darwin tonight or tomorrow. On hearing that, I deflate my newly-bought rubber dinghy - that I spent all of yesterday blowing up - and return it to the shop.

While out, the idea occurs to get on a cruise ship to Asia; not from Darwin, but from somewhere in the south, out of the reach of cyclones. A woman at a travel agency on the high street asks how she can help.

"I'd like to book a cruise, please."

"Where to and when?"

"Anywhere in Australia to anywhere in Asia, leaving anytime in the next month."

"That's kind of vague."

"Also, I only need a one-way ticket, and it needs to be cheap."

She looks at me like I'm an idiot, but after I explain

about the trip, and promise she'll get to play herself in the movie version of it, she does her best to help. After fifteen minutes of searching databases, she finds a Brisbane to Shanghai cruise for £900 that departs next week. But it's fully booked. Most people, she says, book cruises six-to-twelve months in advance, not the week before. After another fifteen minutes of searching, she finds a Sydney to Southampton cruise that has availability. Taking one boat from Australia to the UK would simplify the trip, but at £9,500 it's expensive. I ask for a £8,500 discount. She says no.

With yachts, dinghies, and cruises ruled out, the only option left is to travel from Australia to Asia on a freight ship - the ones transporting cargo around the world. I've heard before that this is possible, but I've never met anyone who's done it. It's one of those, "A friend of a friend's brother-in-law's sister's friend knows someone who might have done it a few years ago," situations. I Google "freight shipping companies in Australia" and find a dozen of them. None mention on their website about taking passengers, but I email all of them anyway.

With that done, and hoping a good deed will swing me some good luck from above, I go to the Red Cross Blood Donor Centre. A nurse there asks me if I lived in the UK between 1980 and1996.

"Yes, for nearly all that time," I tell her.

"We don't accept blood from anyone who spent more than six months in the UK between those dates, due to the risk of mad cow disease."

"Moooooooooooooo."

I offer her my other products, but she doesn't want them either, so I put them back in the Tupperware box and leave.

FREMANTLE

The shipping companies' replies rolled in and weren't positive. One reply, though, had a tip in addition to the knock-back: the guy advised searching for "freighter travel". I did so and found a few companies specialising in booking passengers on freight ships. I contacted them, and now have a Fremantle to Singapore freight ship ticket. Good news, of course, but not ideal: it cost a lot (£1,200), and Fremantle, on the south-west coast near Perth, is 4,000 km from Darwin.

It meant more time on buses, going to the south coast it took me fifty-plus hours to travel up from. I completed a twenty-four-hour bus journey a few days ago, and a thirty-five-hour one today. A wise man would have researched the weather in Darwin before heading there, realised it was impossible to sail at this time of year, and booked himself onto a freight ship departing from Sydney. Alas, a wise man I'm not.

My hostel in Fremantle is more like a halfway house than a backpackers' hostel. The dorm room has yellow-stained walls, a boarded-over fireplace, and a window facing a wall. As I'm assessing how crap it is, Nick, a busker from Melbourne, walks in with something crumpled in his hand.

"It's a sticker with a monkey on it," he says. "I stole it off a train window. It'll look good on my trumpet case. They don't make them like they used to, though. The stickers used to come off real easy."

"Probably they changed the glue to stop people stealing them."

"Yeah, maybe. Life's like that."

In the afternoon, I take a tour of Fremantle Prison, which until twenty years ago was Western Australia's primary maximum security jail. The worst of the worst were sent here.

Steve, the tour guide, takes us inside one of the cells, measuring 2 x 2.5 metres. That's not a lot of space for one person, yet it was two per cell, and they were locked up for sixteen hours a day. Each cell has only a bunk bed, a cupboard, a chair, and a desk. There's no PlayStation, no television, and no toilet. They're shitty but on a par with where I'm staying. If these cells had wifi, I'd rather sleep here.

Steve says despite the cells being terrible, prisoners would prefer to be in them than out in the yard. There were no prison officers in the yard, only ones with guns standing watch over it. Bloody faces and broken bones were suffered everyday; people were raped in the toilets; murders weren't uncommon.

"If you were good-looking, you would be a rape target," Steve says, glancing at me. Is that a compliment? It kind of is. I'll take it as one.

Next, Steve shows us a noose hanging over an open trap-door in the execution room. Forty-plus people were hung at this spot. Steve says he doesn't think any were executed for stealing cows.

When I ask if he used to work at the prison, he refuses to answer. He knows too much to have learnt it from a book, so if he didn't work here, he was a prisoner. Either way, if he offers me a private tour of the toilets, I'll decline.

Back at the hostel, past midnight, I wake to an odd noise. I look down from my top bunk with bleary eyes and see Nick stood swaying. The guy in the other top bunk, Marcel, looks down and says, "Mate, what are you doing?"

There's a mumbled, undecipherable reply.

Marcel adds, "Are you taking a piss? For fuck's sake."

Nick finishes up, then collapses back onto his bed.

Marcel uses his phone as a torch to try to locate the piss, but he can't find it. All goes dark and quiet for five minutes, but Marcel's restless. He gets out his lighter for a second search. This time he finds it: a large pissy patch on the floor in the middle of the room.

If that's not a crime, it should be. Hanging the pisser might be too extreme, but sending him to a far-flung land for seven years of hard labour sounds fair.

INDIAN OCEAN

At Fremantle's North Quay Harbour, a security guard drives me to the ship and, once there, I climb the steep, metal stairs onto the deck. A Filipino man, Bernardo, takes me to a seven-floor structure towards the back of the ship, spanning almost the width of it, which houses the offices, bedrooms, and dining rooms. My room is one of a few kept spare in case a journey requires extra crew. It consists of a lounge, bedroom, and bathroom, and is furnished like a three-star hotel.

Bernardo gives me an information booklet, tells me to wait in my room, then leaves. The booklet looks like it was put together in the mid-nineties when clipart was edgy and exciting, and anyone with Microsoft Publisher was a graphic designer. Images used include bananas, dancers, and flowers - none have any relevance to the page they're on. Reading through, I learn the ship is called MSC Uganda (but is German, not Ugandan). It's 294 metres long, weighs 53,324 tonnes, can hold 4,545 shipping containers, and uses more fuel in a day than the average car owner uses in a lifetime. Those seats make it sound like a beast, yet it's one of the smallest ships at the port.

After six hours of being idle in my room, I get a call on the in-room phone and am told to go to the ship's main office. There, I meet the captain, a German guy in his late-fifties with the face of a wise-wizard. "Welcome aboard, Herr Walters," he says, crushing my fingers with his handshake. He tells me I'm free to go wherever I want on the ship. "You must be careful, though," he adds. "There are many ways you can injure yourself. You can fall over things; things can fall on you. And if you fall into the sea, it's a problem for you, and for us."

He gives me an indemnity form to sign, which says I give up my rights to make any claims against the shipping company, even if they've been negligent.

While walking around, I see a document posted on a wall listing the names and positions of the twenty people working on the ship. It's German brains, Kiribatian brawn: the officers, engineers, and mechanics are all German (except for one Filipino); the deck hands - those doing the hard, dirty work - are all Kiribatian. I've never before heard of Kiribati. It sounds like a made-up country. But the Kiribatians onboard assure me it's real. They claim it's an island nation in the middle of the Pacific Ocean. I'll take their word for it for now, but next time I see a globe, I'll check they're not lying.

I eat meals in the officers' mess-room, in which there are four tables of four. Everyone sits in the same seat each time. They barely speak a word to each other. There are only so many times you can discuss your favourite size and colour of shipping container before the topic gets dull. A waiter serves us food; he calls everyone, including me, "Sir". I've gone from eating own-brand cereal bars in a room whiffing of urine to eating cooked meals served by a waiter in an officers' mess-room. Things are on the up.

After dinner, there's an abandon ship test drill. As instructed in the information booklet, I grab a life jacket and hard hat and head to the port-side lifeboat. I feel smug at being the first one there. Ten minutes later, I feel less smug: someone comes to get me to take me to the other side of the ship. I've been stood at the starboard-side lifeboat.

A spectacled German mechanic tells me, "We don't worry about pirates because of the speed of our ship. The pirates have faster ships, but if the ship they're trying to board is moving quickly, it's difficult for them to get their ladders attached and get onboard."

I'd feel safer if we had some grenades. I guess we could improvise if we had to, using some mouldy potatoes from the kitchen. While not as effective as a grenade, a well-aimed potato can cause a nasty bruise.

At 11 pm, a couple of tugboats latch onto the ship, and the engine starts. I walk out onto the deck for the departure. A few people are stood along the harbour wall, waving ships off. "Goodbye you cow-stealing Aussie bastards," I shout at them. "See you back in the motherland when you've done your time."

After ten minutes, we pass the lighthouse marking the end of the harbour, and we're out at sea. Back in my room, the movement of the ship, lurching side to side, makes me feel sick. I lay in bed trying to sleep, but the creaks, cracks, and whirrs keep me awake long into the night.

The captain said many people get seasick during their first time at sea, and that it can last for days. I don't fancy days of being one lurch away from spewing over a passing Kiribatian, but we're too far from shore for me to swim back.

I've given up looking out the windows in my room. There's nothing to see but sea. They should have invested the money spent on windows on wifi instead. Maybe it's not the cost of the technology that's the problem, but restrictions on extra weight. Giving in-room internet to a ship of lonely men, at sea for months at a time, would require several tonnes of tissues to be stocked onboard.

With no porn or TV, I resort to going for a walk. The barriers bordering the ship's outer edge are only half a metre high, and the walkway is no more than a metre wide. I nudge myself along at a pace only marginally faster than stationary, taking ten minutes to reach the bow. After singing *My Heart Will Go On*, I'm eager to return to my room. Partly because I could die out here, and partly because I'm wearing trainers - borrowed from one of the crew to adhere to health and safety regulations. I don't like wearing trainers. It's like putting a child in a cage. For half an hour it's ok, but any longer is cruel.

In the afternoon, it's land ahoy! We pass between jungle-covered Indonesian islands. The one on the left is Sumatra, the one on the right is Java. Sitting on a deck chair, with tropical islands either side of me, the sun on my face and the wind in my hair, I think to myself that this is the life, this is why I'm not settling down and being a boring bastard.

Since I turned thirty a year ago, I've had an increasing amount of people asking, "Mark, don't you think it's time you settled down?" Invariably, these people have never been anything but settled. They've lived their lives in one town. They married a local, got a mortgage, and are part way through a fifty-year slog of doing a job they don't like. Turning the question around on them, asking when they're going to unsettle, is met with a blank stare, a look of confusion. The way I see it, most people live until they're about eighty, and those years should be split between being settled and being unsettled. Eighty divided by two equates to forty years of each. So it mathematically makes sense not to settle until you're forty. You can't argue with maths.

A few hours later, I go to the ship's control room - or "bridge", as us seafaring souls call it. In it is a steering wheel thingy (not the official nautical name); a large control panel, containing hundreds of buttons and dials; and three monitors - two showing radars and one a map. The map is incredibly detailed. In comparison, Google Maps resembles something drawn by a three-year-old. It shows not only where the land is, but sea depths and danger points. I note we've detoured around an area marked "Explosives Dumping Ground".

Bernardo is currently controlling the ship. "It runs on autopilot except when near land or passing through a busy shipping lane," he tells me. "Even when on autopilot, though, we need to keep an eye on the speed and reduce it if there are large waves or swells, to prevent damage to the ship or containers falling off. Problems are rare but do happen. At my previous company, during a severe storm, we lost three tiers of containers."

Afterwards, I visit the gym, pool, and sauna. Don't think this is a luxury liner, though: the pool is a three-square-metre metal box filled with seawater, the gym has only three pieces of antiquated weight-lifting equipment, and the sauna is the size of a fat man's coffin. If you want to exercise properly, the only option is to run in circles - small circles because there's not space to run in big ones. The crew likely go months at a time without any decent exercise, which, along with the stodgy food, explains their sizeable bellies. It's a cooped up existence, and one I'd struggle with. They get paid well and aren't stressed or overworked, but the boredom must take its toll. They don't even get to see the places the ship goes to, as they have to work the whole time the ship is docked.

In the evening, a barbecue takes place on on F Deck, the top floor of the ship. With today being my thirty-first birthday, I head up there fearing I may be in for some high jinks. I wonder what they have in mind. Walking the plank? A mermaid stripper? Sucking off an octopus? It times like these you need Google. Google would know how sailors celebrate birthdays.

There are no planks, mermaids, or octopi waiting for me, though. The crew always have a barbecue on Tuesday evenings, and no one cares that it's my birthday. There's not even a balloon - not a single, bloody one. When no one's looking, I slip my speech into the bin.

At 1.30 am an alarm sounds around the ship and the phone in my room rings. The captain says a Singaporean immigration officer is onboard and wants to see me. I grab my bag and go to the ship's office, where the officer stamps me into the country without asking any questions, like, "Why the heck are you arriving on a freight ship?!"

A local in the ship's office selling sim cards to the crew says he'll drive me into the city centre for £15. Ten minutes later I'm sat in a van with him, weaving through the streets of Singapore. He drops me at the Hawaii Hostel. The receptionist is asleep across the check-in desk. After waking him, he takes me to a grim box room, lacking any windows.

Straight away, I'm on the internet. In the past week, I've had no news from beyond the ship. I might have missed the arrival of a new Messiah or the invention of teleportation. I'd take the latter over the former. Nothing significant or exciting has happened, though. It's the same old, boring, blah, blah, blah stories about people killing each other.

As I lie in bed, I think back over the trip so far. At the outset, I thought it might take a month to reach Singapore, and I would come via East Timor and/or Indonesia. I was wrong on both counts: it's taken me eight weeks, and I didn't step foot in either of those countries.

I also miscalculated how much I'd spend getting here. I've spent four times more than expected.

From here on, I need to travel faster and cheaper.

SINGAPORE

I leave the Hawaii Hostel at daybreak. The new place I find is called The Pod, a "Boutique Capsule Hotel". The beds are boxed in on all but one side. If you think that sounds quite a lot like I'll be sleeping in a cupboard, you're right. However much they try to dress it up - and they have, with a light, hangers, and fold-out table - it's basically a cupboard. At £30 a night, it's not a cheap one either.

I head out to explore the city, not knowing where I'm going or what I'll see. Exploring new places is what I most enjoy in life. My senses sucking up the sights, sounds, and smells, my mind broadening. It's what makes the pains of travelling - like sleeping in a cupboard - worth it.

Near the yacht-filled water at Raffles Place, I take a ride on the Singapore Flyer, the world's tallest Ferris wheel. In the queue, I see a sign saying the wheel weighs the same as 437.8 elephants, and the safety net under it can withstand twenty-five elephants falling from a two-storey building. Imagine if everything was measured in terms of elephants:

on medical forms, you'd write you're one-fifth of an elephant tall; at supermarkets, you'd ask for an elephant's toe of bananas; at work, you'd get a monthly salary of three elephants.

From the wheel, I see shiny skyscrapers everywhere. With so much scraping, there's barely any sky left. Because the country spans only 687 km², they've had to build up instead of out. That building has been done fast, funded by Singapore establishing itself as the financial headquarters of South Asia. It's been a meteoric rise for the once sleepy colonial outpost, which only gained independence from Britain in 1965.

It's not all skyscrapers, though. Fifty-plus parks and four nature reserves make Singapore as green as it is glass. Gardens By The Bay is one of Singapore's green-fingered projects. It consists of two huge glass domes and an outdoor area called Supertree Grove. In the latter are Avatar-like tree structures acting as vertical gardens; the inside and outside of their towering purple trunks bursting with vivid flora. The Flower Dome maintains a constant spring day climate and is split into eight sections based on regions of the world, each displaying plant-life from the respective region. It's the type of thing we'll be living in on Mars when we've cocked up the earth. The second dome, Cloud Forest, resembles a lost world. Within it is a mountain-like structure, on one side of which is the world's largest indoor waterfall. It's over-grown with otherworldly plants covering the spectrum of colours. If I'd brought my Avatar costume with me, now would be the time to wear it. But it was one of the sacrifices made when opting to travel light. It was either pack my

Avatar costume or pack more than one pair of boxers. I've dropped a clanger there because I've not needed more than one pair of boxers.

In a different part of the city are the Singapore Botanic Gardens, home to ten thousand species of plant. It includes an area of rainforest, part of the original vegetation that covered Singapore before the skyscrapers soared. Its VIP Orchid Garden operates a hybridisation programme to create new species of orchids. When famous people visit, an unnamed plant is pulled from a cupboard and named after them. As a result, there are beautiful flowers tainted with unfortunate names like Dendrobium Margaret Thatcher. A sign says: "Outstanding hybrids from the orchid breeding programme have been used to promote goodwill and foster closer ties between nations since 1956." Singapore hasn't been involved in any wars since then so it must be working. America, take note: divert military money from missiles to orchids.

Among the skyscrapers and greenery are malls - a lot of them. I've lost count of how many I've been in today. They're hard to avoid. Every metro exit leads into one, and the exits from one mall take you directly to the next. More than ten line Orchard Road. Each would be the shopping pinnacle in most cities, but here is just another notch on the credit card. Marc Jacobs, Hugo Boss, Armani, Cartier, and Prada have all doubled-up on stores. The abundance of high-end boutiques is because there's demand for them. Singapore ranks in the top fifteen in the world for average monthly salary and has more millionaires per capita than any other country. There's much financial disparity, though. Singapore has no minimum wage or social welfare system. £2.50 per day is what nearly 400,000 Singaporeans have left after paying for rent, utilities, and healthcare. You can't buy much here with £2.50 a day. Not even a Prada button.

You have to show your passport in Singapore when buying medicine, and they keep a nationwide database of everyone's pharmaceutical purchases. Included in the database are tourists. It results in me being interrogated at a pharmacy while trying to buy anti-histamine tablets.

"You already bought these. Why do you want more?"

"I bought one pack. I've decided I want one more."

"It's too much."

"They're pills to stop me sneezing. I'm not asking for methadone."

"Methadone? Why are you talking about methadone?"

"I'm not asking for it. I'm putting things in perspective."

"Maybe you have a problem with drugs."

I tell her to forget it; that I'll go to one of the traditional Chinese medicine stores and buy dried donkey testicles to block my nostrils.

I didn't force the issue with the pharmacist, in case she put my name on a blacklist. Singapore isn't a country you want to be on such a list. They have some of the strictest drug laws in the world. Getting caught with a sizeable amount results in the death penalty. The law applies to foreigners as well as locals. You get hanged the Friday following your sentencing.

It's even illegal to import or sell chewing gum. Though, that only gets you caned instead of hung. Caning is a standard punishment used for minor offences like vandalism or petty theft. Littering or spitting gets you a £240 fine, putting it on a par with not flushing a public toilet after use.

In the evening, I try to find Singapore's underbelly. It can't all be as squeaky clean as I've seen so far. I want to peek behind the curtain, where the half a million paupers hang out. According to Google, Geylang is where I'll find them. At a metro station, I ask how to get to Geylang, which doesn't have a station. "Which part Geylang? What do there?" the ticket seller asks me.

"I don't know which part. I just want to walk around."

"Go there for find woman?"

"No, just to look around."

"Go Aljunied Station. Have woman near there."

"No, but, I don't..."

"Move along. More people waiting."

Geylang is indeed another side to Singapore. It's skanky, with trash on the ground, tatty shops and cafes, and an assortment of scruffs and pissheads. There are rundown houses with their numbers in red lights. They must be brothels, or at least happy ending massage places. I'm surprised Singapore's goody, goody government allow it. 10% discount cards for ministers, perhaps.

I visit a "hawker centre" for dinner, a canteen-style building filled with former pushcart vendors that the government mopped up as part of their street clean-up initiative. At one of these places you can have Chinese noodle soup for breakfast, Malay curry for lunch, Indian biryani for dinner and, if you're a greedy bastard, a burger for supper. And for less than £10 in total. I'm not ordering any of those dishes, though; I'm eating braised pig trotter.

It's mostly bone and fat, but there are a couple of chunks of edible meat. Halfway through the meal, someone tells me, "Your chopstick upside down." In Asia, this is looked upon like an Asian in Europe using a knife and fork upside down. You would think someone using a knife and fork upside down was an idiot. Today, I am that idiot.

Looking for dessert, I pass a stall selling durian, a large fruit with a green, spiky outer shell and a yellow, fleshy inside. I've seen signs on the metro and in elevators saying "No durians allowed". I thought that strange, but find out why after buying a portion. The plastic gloves they give me to eat it with should have made me wary. It stinks of vomit. It tastes of vomit too. After two bites, my gag reflex kicks in, and I chuck it. The lesson learnt: don't buy food that's banned in enclosed spaces and requires the wearing of gloves.

On the metro on the way back, a fart forces itself out, which I blame on the durian. Farting on the metro must be illegal in Singapore. I'll be fined, caned, and hung for my heinous crime. I have only one choice: become a fugitive and go on the run to Malaysia.

MALAYSIA

KUALA LUMPUR

I cross the bridge that connects Singapore to Johor Bahru in Malaysia and enter the country on a ninety-day visa-on-arrival. The bus station there is a bustling, manic place. In the forecourt is a constantly changing line-up of fifty-plus fancifully coloured buses, in states ranging from dilapidated to plush. The destination signs in the front windows display exotic-sounding places like Negeri Sembilan, Selangor, and Melaka. At a couple of dozen counters lined along the front of the station, swarms of shabby guys tout tickets, harassing everyone who passes. I scout for the most religious-looking ticket seller, thinking they'll be least likely to overcharge me. They won't risk a stint in the eternal hellfire so they can rinse me of a few extra ringgit. I spot a woman in a head-scarf, with worry lines so deep that they must be the result of living in constant trepidation of displeasing an imaginary overlord in the clouds. She'll do.

"I'd like a ticket to Kuala Lumpur, please. How much is it? Is the bus nice?"

"Ticket is £6. Bus is super nice."

She points, straight-faced, to a photo of the bus, which has "Super Nice" written on the side of it. It's the name of the bus company.

On arrival in Kuala Lumpur, I book into the Cube Hotel for £17 per night. It's a bona fide hotel, though not quite a Hilton. My room is larger than a cupboard but doesn't have any windows. I'm staying here because I need to do some online work to replenish my bank account. It will require some quiet time, which is in short supply at hostels. I can earn money while in bed. Don't jump to conclusions. I'm not a webcam boy, stripping for perverts. I'm a search engine optimisation consultant, helping businesses rank their websites higher in Google. With a laptop and wifi, I can work from anywhere.

My hotel is in Bukit Bintang, the most touristy area of the city. But even here there aren't many tourists because Kuala Lumpur isn't a tourist hotspot. With Bangkok to the north and Singapore to the south, Kuala Lumpur is the middle child, often overlooked. The vibe is distinctly different to the Chinese-tinged international one in Singapore. It feels more like Asia. The dirt, noise, and disorder levels are several notches higher. The showcase landmark looming over the skyline is a 450-metre space-age-looking behemoth: the Petronas Towers. From 1998 to 2004, it was the world's tallest building, and it remains the tallest twin towers. An impressive feat for a country outside the top thirty largest in the world.

A large mall, Suria KLCC, forms the base of the towers. Even in this, Kuala Lumpur's main mall, half the toilets are of the squat variety - a doored cubicle around a hole in the floor. I've used squatters in the past. It's a stressful experience every time. Crouched over the chasm, your knees crack and creak. You wobble every which way as you try to balance without touching any surfaces. Beads of sweat stream over your face as try to hit the oh-so-small hole, knowing the slightest miscalculation of angle will result in the nightmare scenario of dropping one into the jeans around your ankles. With the deed done, you have to find a way to adequately clean yourself, using not tissue paper but either a hose pipe or a bowl of water. I'll be getting a lot of practice at this. From here until Europe, at least half the toilets I come across will be squat ones. I haven't ruled out the stress-free option of wearing nappies.

From the mall, I go to the 420-metre KL Tower. It makes more sense to go up this than the taller Petronas Towers so that I can see them from here. After paying, a woman hands me a form and says, "You must sign this before you can go up."

"Sign a form? What for?"

"Every September, base jumpers come here. You must sign to say you're not a base jumper. Base jumping is only ok in September. Please, don't jump today."

"Do you get many base jumpers going up in flip-flops and without a parachute?"

"No."

I sign the form. What a waste of a sheet of paper.

Afterwards, I wait thirty minutes for a train at KL Sentral

Station to take me to Batu Caves. Thirty seconds after boarding the train, I realise everyone else in the carriage is a woman. I notice a sign saying the carriage is only for women. I jump back onto the platform. The next carriage is women only too, and the one after that. The train doors shut. It leaves without me. Waiting for the next train, I note that about a third of each train passing through is for women only. Ladies, you can have the vote or your own train carriages, but not both.

At Batu Caves, steep steps climb a rock face, past a golden statue of Murugan, a Hindu deity. There are 272 steps to reach the temple inside the cave at the top. I buy a can of Red Bull to help me climb the steps but soon regret it. My heart pounds like an amphetamine-fuelled bongo player. At the top, strobes of sunlight bathe the temple through an opening above. Beside it, some idiots have tainted the holy vibe with a shop. I don't know why anyone would climb 272 steps into a mystical cave to buy a flashing picture frame or a "Hinduism way of life" car sticker. Cock-a-doodle-doos echo from unseen chickens. And there are monkeys. Everywhere. People think monkeys are cute, but uncaged ones aren't. The one Ross had in Friends is the exception, not the rule. They'll bite and scratch and, given a chance, will steal candy from a baby. One leaps onto a girl's backpack. She screams. The monkey grabs a water bottle from the side of the bag, then races off. Another steals a bottle of Gatorade straight from a guy's hand. Once they've drunk their plunder, they toss the bottles on the ground; so they're litterers as well as thieves. Next time I'm online, I'll be making donations to NASA and L'Oreal.

At night, while putting off doing work, I check Facebook for the seventeenth time in an hour and find out my niece has just been born. I'm now, for the first time, an uncle. I Google "how to be an uncle" to see what it entails. It's relatively straightforward. My primary duties are stopping her Dad from embarrassing her in front of her friends, and getting her drunk when she turns eighteen. One of those will be easy; the other will be impossible.

I decide to send her a postcard. Sending one is almost the same as being there in person.

"Hello, Chloe. Welcome to the world. It's not perfect, but it's not too bad. For the first years, you can get away with watching cartoons. When you start learning, I recommend the alphabet. It comes in useful from time to time."

At the post office, it costs only £0.09 to send the postcard to the UK. Is it going by carrier pigeon? Will they throw it in the air when it's windy and hope for the best? Or will they put it in the bin, knowing that by the time I realise it hasn't been sent, I'll be long gone from Kuala Lumpur?

GEORGE TOWN

UNESCO typically give world heritage status to specific buildings or sites, but they've given it to the whole of George Town, on the island of Penang in the north-west of the country, 350 km from Kuala Lumpur. I can see why: it's like stepping back in time. Its eclectic mishmash of architecture draws on colonial and Asian influences from the past three centuries, combing to create scenes fit for a movie set. Singapore was like this before money rolled in and skyscrapers shot up. Money will change a place, and not always for the better.

I stumble upon a market on some dusty ground on Lebuh Armenian. A couple of dozen people have each laid out a plastic sheet to display their tat on. And it really is tat - beyond second-hand and onto third, fourth, and fifth. Despite the paucity of anything of use or value, buyers scrutinise objects like they're buying a diamond. One seller's wares consist of a rusty tin, a light switch, a piece of rope, a pot lid (no pot), a used paintbrush, a book (in Russian), a certificate for something, a half-used tube of metal glue, a World Cup '82 plastic whistle, and a KFC alarm clock (batteries not included).

Down by the water at Weld Quay are villages on wooden piers, a stone's throw apart. Each belongs to a different clan: Chew, Yeoh, Koay, Tan, Lim, and Lee. In the nineteenth century, Chinese immigrants arriving in Penang would join one of these clans to help establish themselves in their new country. Fishing was the money maker, and the clans would battle each other for the best spots to fish from. It was like *Game Of Thrones*, but with more fish. The descendants of the original settlers still live here, on their respective piers, in creaky shacks. They let tourists walk on the piers so they can sell them snacks, using the funds to augment their arsenal, so they can finally eliminate their nuisance neighbours and reign supreme on the fishy throne.

In the centre of town, hordes of groovy gangs congregate around tables outside cafes, smoking roll-ups and reciting chapters from *Lonely Planet*. They wear baggy, cotton trousers; vests emblazoned with "Same, same but different" or "Beer Lao"; and brightly coloured, thick-rimmed sunglasses. Every sentence uttered includes "like" or "amazing". I saw few of them in Kuala Lumpur or Singapore. This is a Thai visa-run hotspot, though. Groovy gangers leave their Thai beach paradise the day before their visa expires to come here for a few days to get a new Thai visa.

I need to use a Thai visa service myself. While I can get a fifteen-day visa-on-arrival for Thailand at the border, that won't be long enough for me. I'd like to get visas for Myanmar, India, and China from their respective embassies in Bangkok, which will take more than fifteen days because obtaining visas is often a time-sucking, frustrating nightmare. Fortunately, the need for pre-arranging a visa should be limited to only half a dozen countries on this trip. Having a UK passport means I've effectively won the passport lottery. No other nationality gets more visa-free and visa-on-arrival access to other countries.

After lunch, I grab a street art map of the town. Over the past few years, more and more street art has been added, and there are currently twenty-plus pieces spread about. I've seen some without actively trying to find it but finding it all requires a map because most of it isn't in obvious places. It's like an Easter egg hunt, though not at Easter and without any eggs. Not that I've done one of those before. My parents put my Easter eggs on the kitchen table. If they hid them in the garden, I'd have called the NSPCC. A typical piece is a large painting on a wall, given a 3D feel by incorporating real-life features, like a window or motorcycle. It ranges from the mundane (cats) to the cultural (a street scene) to the wacky (Bruce Lee kung-fu kicking cats). Some pieces, via an accompanying description, say something about the street or building they adorn or offer an insight into Penang's way of life. One highlights where Jimmy Choo - who was born in Penang - undertook his shoemaking apprenticeship. He made his first pair when he was eleven years old, which makes me feel lazy. I'm thirty-one, and I haven't made any yet.

Later, I flag down one of George Town's ubiquitous time-worn trishaws. There's one wheel at the back, above which the driver sits to peddle; and two at the front, either side of a seat for two people (or one American). The driver is a sixty-something-year-old man. As he peddles me around, I feel somewhere between a colonial master surveying the empire, and a toddler in a pushchair. Progress is slow. He's not even getting close to the speed limit. I'm tempted to whip him like a horse with my earphone cable to quicken his pace. But there are too many groovy gangers around, and they're liberal-types, likely to report me to Amnesty International. The pre-agreed price was £4 for thirty minutes, but I put an end to his misery, and mine, after twenty and decide to walk instead. It's a shame he performed poorly. It was such good value I was considering hiring him to take me all the way back to London. Having done the calculations, though, at the speed we were going I'd have missed my niece's eighteenth birthday.

Back at the hostel, I see on the news that a plane going from Kuala Lumpur to Beijing is missing, thought to have crashed into the sea. There are no flight crash worries for me on this trip, but a road accident isn't unlikely. Malaysia and Thailand are road death hotspots, both making the top twenty in the list of countries with the most road fatalities per year, per hundred thousand inhabitants. Thailand is fourth on the list, with thirty-eight per hundred thousand. In comparison, the UK has four per hundred thousand.

I speak to a Chilean staying in the same room as me. He recently went to Myanmar and tells me, "There are restrictions on where you can go, and they change week to week. There are many army checkpoints, and if they don't want you to go to a particular place, they'll kick you off the bus. Myanmar's border with Bangladesh is closed. Its borders with India and China are technically open, but you need special permits to cross them. As a foreigner, you've no chance of getting one."

I had in mind taking a route that went via Myanmar, but I'll have to scrap that. I don't want to hit a dead-end in Myanmar and have to backtrack into Thailand. Travelling from Thailand to Laos to China makes the most sense.

THAILAND

AO NANG

Last night, after a day in the nondescript Hat Yai, I arrived by mini-van in Ao Nang, a coastal town in the south-western province of Krabi. The driver seemed to be engaged in an unofficial attempt to break the world record for most people in a mini-van. There were seats for fifteen people, but through knee-sitting and creative limb-positioning, he crammed in twenty-five. If we'd had an accident - not unlikely based on the manic driving - paramedics would have been pulling people out for days, like a twisted version of a magician pulling rabbits from a top hat.

Today, on Ao Nang's white sand beach, fifty-plus long-tail boats line the shore, bobbing up and down with coloured cloth tied around their bows, on which their captains sit, beaming bright smiles beneath dark aviators. It costs £2 for the ten-minute ride to Railay, a peninsula accessible only by sea. Crossing the emerald water, passing thick jungle, sheer-faced cliffs, and in-sea rock formations, I'm reminded of the fly-in helicopter scenes from Jurassic Park, and half expect to see a T-Rex sunbathing on the sand.

At Railay, I wander around its four beaches: West Railay, for the moneyed wanting a slice of luxury; East Railay, for the cheapskates wanting a fruit shake and pancake; Phra Nang, for the everyman wanting to swim and lounge; and Ton Sai, for the cool kids wanting to rock climb and toke. While foreigners are in their skimpies, with thunder thighs and moobs on display, locals keep as covered as possible to avoid getting tanned, because they consider light skin more attractive than dark. They look in bemusement at foreigners laying in the sun, ravaging their lovely white skin. Dumbfounded foreigners look back at them sat in the shade applying skin-whitening products.

Like the Thais, I keep myself covered, but for a different reason. Wearing shirts, jeans, and flip-flops every day has given me ludicrous-looking tan lines. My face, arms, and feet are all brown, while the rest of me is white. Except for my willy, which is light brown, because sometimes I walk about with it hanging out of my jeans.

On a path through the jungle between the beaches, I see a tree with a hundred-plus flip-flops nailed to it. A sign says: "The flip-flops on this tree were collected around Ton Sai in twenty-six minutes in the 2013 flip-flop-athon. What do you consider rubbish?" It breaks my heart that these flip-flops were abandoned. People buy them impulsively, thinking them cool and fun. Then, after a couple of weeks, as their holiday draws to a close, the prospect of wearing them to the office dawns on them, and so, under cover of darkness, they bury them in the sand. It's cruelty of the worst kind, an inexcusable act. Flip-flops are for life, not just for holidays.

After cheering myself up with an ice cream, I take a long-tail boat to Hong Island for a kayaking tour. On the tour - led by Jay, a Thai guy - are four Singaporean couples and two Thai women. Each kayak can fit one to three people, and there are twelve people in total, so it should be two people per kayak. The Thai women, however, say they need Jay to paddle for them, which means, not wanting to play gooseberry on a Singaporean kayak, I have to go solo. No problem, I think, reasoning that the women might slow the men if they don't pull their weight or co-ordinate their paddling. Based on this, I propose a race, with a penalty for the loser: they have to kayak around the island again.

I regret this ten minutes later when my arms are aching, and I'm lagging far behind everyone else. I think my women-are-deadweight-on-kayaks theory might be bollocks, and I might be a sexist wanker. Jay shouts back at me, "Come on, man. Why so slow? Long way go yet. Thirty minute more. Go faster." I feel bad now for slagging off my pensioner-aged Malaysian trishaw driver.

I complete the loop of the island but lose the race - no photo finish required. I'm reminded the loser has to go around again. But Jay comes to my rescue: "No, no, no. He not go again. I never see someone this slow. I want go home my wife now. Not want wait two hour more for him."

Back at Ao Nang, German, Russian, and Scandinavian

couples and families eat spaghetti, steaks, and tacos at air-conditioned, glass-fronted restaurants, with names like Eden, Roma, and Gringos. And Indian suit-sellers line the road, trying to shake the hand of every passerby: "Hello, my friend. Suit very nice. Please, yes, thank you." It could be any tourist resort, anywhere.

There's one noticeable difference, though: the massage shops (happy endings optional) and girlie bars (everything optional). Outside them, women sit like a harem, preening, gossiping, and giggling. "Handsome, sexy man, you want massage?" they say to me as I pass. It's good for your ego being called sexy and handsome, but the shine is taken off when you realise they call every guy that, even those as sexy and handsome as Danny DeVito.

It's mostly women offering the "services", but there are also gay men and men dressed as women. I don't see any women dressed as men, but if that's what you want, and you're willing to pay, someone would meet your need, because anything goes in Thailand. It reminds me of Blur's *Girls & Boys*:

> *"Girls who are boys,*
> *Who like boys to be girls,*
> *Who do boys like they're girls,*
> *Who do girls like they're boys,*
> *Always should be someone you really love."*

But in Thailand you don't have to love them; you just have to give them £20.

Some guys coming to Thailand worry about pulling a ladyboy. It's an easy mistake to make - especially if inebriated - because many Thai ladyboys look and act so feminine that they make half of Western girls look like guys. I say, if you can't tell the difference, you may as well take a chance. You know how the saying goes: "If it looks like a duck, swims like a duck, and quacks like a duck, then shag the duck."

A kilometre down the road from the beach, there's less of a Costa Del Thai vibe. I find a market selling cheap Thai food. For £1, I buy a portion of rice and grilled beef cooked in herbs and spices. It comes in two small bags, which I take back to my room to eat. Once there, I realise there's no plate or cutlery. The solution: tip one bag into the other and use a bottle top as a spoon. This works better than you think it would. Try it at your next dinner party to cut down on washing-up.

There's no solution, though, for the power cut. Sitting in the dark, scooping food into my mouth with a bottle top, I wonder if I should have just had a taco at Gringos.

BANGKOK

I arrive in Bangkok, or to give it its full, official name: Krungthepmahanakhon Amonrattanakosin Mahintharayutthaya Mahadilokphop Noppharatratchathaniburirom Udomratchaniwetmahasathan Amonphimanawatansathit Sakkathattiyawitsanukamprasit. It's tempting to use that to fluff up my word count, but for your sake, I'll stick to Bangkok.

I travelled here on a first-class bus, sat beside a shaven-headed monk wearing orange robes. I thought it wasn't very monk-like to take the first-class bus when there were cheaper second-class ones. And he was drinking Sprite, not water. If he's serious about being a monk, he should have walked and drunk his own piss.

After finding a hostel, I visit Wat Pho, a complex of temples and shrines. The signature piece is a forty-five-metre golden statue of Buddha lying on one side - built that way, I assume, to save on scaffolding costs. Lined along the statue are fifty metal pots. The deal is you pay £0.30 for fifty coins, then place a coin in each pot, making a wish each time. Fifty wishes for £0.30 is great value. At that price, I'll be happy if even one of them comes true. To be the safe side, I make the same wish fifty times: not to have got an STD in Ao Nang.

The back of Wat Pho, away from the masses making bargain wishes by the lazy Buddha, is peaceful and relaxing; incense lingers in the air, the chants of monks echo. I sit down under a tree, resolute that I won't stand until I'm enlightened. Thirty minutes later, I stand; not enlightened, but suffering from pins and needles. I've got time yet, though. Buddha became enlightened at thirty-five years old. I'm only thirty-one; I still have four years to beat him. Though, perhaps approaching enlightenment as a competition isn't an enlightened way to do it.

Because of Bangkok's legendary traffic jams, it takes an age to get back to the hostel. A journey that, based on distance, should take ten minutes can in Bangkok take three to ten times that. The near-permanent gridlock is a result of vast swathes of the city not being accessible by either metro or monorail, for which there are only three lines and fifty or so stations for a population of eight million. London, which has a similar number of people, has a metro network of eleven lines and two-hundred and seventy stations.

After lunch, I spend two tedious hours filling in my Chinese visa application form. China is one of the countries that doesn't give visa-free or visa-on-arrival access to UK citizens. We stole Hong Kong and flooded their country with opium, but that was ages ago. Come on, China, get over it.

As well as a completed application form, the following are required:

- A detailed day-by-day itinerary.
- Hotel booking confirmations.
- Inbound and outbound plane tickets.

I plot a route to take me through a few Chinese cities and into Kazakhstan; note down tourist-related sights and activities in those cities; find train times that fit with the route; and book hostels on booking.com, which offers a free cancellation policy. The plane tickets requirement, I'll have to explain myself out of at the embassy.

Inside the drab, grey visa wing of the embassy, I take a ticketed number, sit on one of the plastic chairs, and settle in for a long wait, feeling worried. I'm screwed if I don't get this visa. If I can't travel through China, I'll have to either pass from Myanmar into India - which I've been told is as good as impossible - then get a boat from India to somewhere in the Middle East; or get a boat from Thailand to Russia. The latter might be possible but would likely cost three or four times more than the boat from Australia to Singapore. My funds won't cover that cost.

When it's my turn, I go to the counter and push my wad of papers through a hole in the glass, so low I have to bend nearly ninety degrees to talk through it. The short, stout Chinese woman on the other side, who speaks abruptly in broken English, spends a couple of minutes looking through the papers then quizzes me on my work status and lack of flights. She's satisfied with my answers but throws an unexpected spanner in the works. "Xinjiang province, next Kazakhstan, have problem now with China central government," she says. "If you want go Xinjiang province, you must letter invitation from Xinjiang province government. No letter invitation, you no get China visa."

"How can I get a letter of invitation from the Xinjiang province government?"

"You must to contact them. Phone. Email. Up to you. Not our problem."

"Do you have contact details for them?"

"You want, you find. I tell you already, it not our problem."

There's no hope of me getting that letter of invitation. I imagine a phone call with someone at the office of the Xinjiang province government going like this:

"Hello, I would like a letter of invitation."

"Nee hoh bin chow mein ha."

"Does anyone there speak English?"

"Englishe? Ga woo kin gan gooley gooley gooley gooley gooley kin gan ga."

"Can I get a letter of invitation?"

"Eh? Pren crackey?"

"No, not prawn crackers. A letter of invitation."

"Me no noey you. Fucky offy."

I leave the embassy and consider my options: I can avoid Xinjiang by going through China into Mongolia then Russia; or lie about my route on the visa application, go through Xinjiang on my way to Kazakhstan, and hope no one checks on me while I'm there, realises I'm somewhere I'm not supposed to be, and locks me up or deports me.

I've reworked my visa application for a route taking me through China into Mongolia. I don't know if I'll follow that route or not, but I can wait until I get to the city of Chengdu in central China before making a final decision. From there I can either head north towards Mongolia or go westwards, via Xinjiang, towards Kazakhstan - the more direct, cheaper option.

At the embassy, I deal with a different woman at the counter, who after looking through my application asks to see my visa for Mongolia. I explain I haven't got it yet; that there's no point getting it if I can't get a Chinese visa. She inspects my paperwork again, then hands me a pink slip and says to come back next week to collect the visa. It's progress, but the visa still needs to be signed-off by someone higher up the chain, who may want to see train tickets - not just dates and times - and/or a Mongolian visa. Both of those are doable, though, if necessary.

Later, at the hostel, I hear chanting, cheering, and amplified speeches coming from outside, and go to investigate what the fuss is about. Thousands of people stream along the road, waving Thai flags, blowing whistles, and holding placards. It's a diverse crowd: bent-backed, elderly women walk beside butch men wearing balaclavas, and spectacled, uniformed students are arm in arm with slickly-dressed business-types. On hearing the commotion, more and more people appear from side streets and inside shops, offices, and restaurants, to stand roadside and show their support. Others, in the windows of buildings and office blocks, poke out their heads to bellow their backing. A Thai man next to me says, "These people not like Thai government. This Saturday, at Lumphini Park, will be more than a hundred thousand people. This government will end."

The leader of the opposition party, who I recognise from TV and newspapers, walks past a couple of metres in front of me. People clamour to get close and shake his hand or snap a photo. I take it as my cue to leave. This is their protest, not mine. Plus, I don't want to get caught up in any naughtiness. Thais are renowned as friendly people who avoid confrontation, but the divide on this issue is deep and has resulted in shots being fired, and even grenades being thrown, at similar protests in Bangkok recently. Politics, eh? What a palaver. Constant complaining and fighting with it, no politicians to blame for your problems without it.

In the afternoon, I visit Sarn Pantai Norasing Temple
with Yui, a Thai friend of mine - not of the pay-per-hour
variety - from a previous visit to Thailand. I feel like a div
being at temples as a tourist, while locals are doing their
rituals. They're trying to make a spiritual connection, while
I'm nosing around, looking gormless. I don't feel such a div
today, though, because I'm not convinced it's a genuine
temple. Outside and inside are hundreds of garishly
coloured chicken statues, ranging in size from tiny to larger
than me. I guess a monk bought them on a whim via
Amazon when they were on special offer: buy one large
chicken statue, get a hundred small ones free.

"I don't think this is a real temple," I say to Yui.

"It real temple, for sure. It not fake temple."

"There's a simple test that can be used to decide."

"Really? What test?"

"If a temple has more statues of chickens than Buddha,
it's fake."

I regret this on the way out when I smack my big toe on
a rock in the car park. Bloody Karma.

At Chatuchak market, Bangkok's largest one, they've got
everything you could want, plus a lot of crap you don't, and
they've got it cheap. You just need to find it, and that's not
easy. It's so vast they hand out maps at the entrance to help
you find your way around. It's hard to read a map, though,
when you're dazed and dehydrated and jammed in an alley
the width of two slim Thai people. People sweat, barge, and
argue as they shop for handcrafted wooden frogs and "I
Sucked Cock In Bangkok" t-shirts.

I've had enough of the place after five minutes, but

can't leave without seeing the infamous animal section of the market. They've got cats, dogs, pigs, rabbits, parrots, chickens, monkeys, peacocks, chipmunks, and a whole host of other furry and feathered critters too. I'm tempted to buy a monkey so I can plaster it with make-up and catapult it into space, but they're expensive. A baby pig is more affordable. It could be a companion for long bus rides, keep me warm on cold nights. But it's challenging enough to get myself a Chinese visa; getting one for a porker would be even more troublesome. I'd only go through that much trouble for a donkey, and only then if it were a pretty one.

The conditions for most of the animals are cramped and filthy. They have no direct sunlight, yet have to put up with temperatures of thirty-five-plus degrees. Some look dead, or on the verge of it, lying on their backs with eyes closed and barely breathing. "If animal get sick," Yui says, "let them die. Cheaper for get new than pay vet bill."

In the evening, I take a tuk-tuk to Khao San Road, the backpacker hub of Bangkok, where groovy gangers gather. There are no posh hotels here; only simple rooms of questionable cleanliness, for as cheap as £5 a night. Hair-braiders, tattoo artists, and the like are out in force. There are even more Indian suit sellers than there were in Ao Nang. It seems like a lost cause trying to sell suits to guys who haven't washed their underwear since last month. From behind a rack of naff t-shirts, a fortune-teller pounces. "Mister," he says, "I can look your palm and tell your future."

"If you look at my palm, you'll tell me my future is to wash my hands."

"Really, mister, if I look your palm I can see many thing. Even name your mother."

"I'm not paying you to tell me the name of my mother. I already know it."

Among the clothes and tourist knick-knacks on offer are knives, tasers, and XXX DVDs. And pharmaceuticals too: "Sale: Valium 1.0, Oral Jelly, Cialis, Kamagra & Viagra. Prescription not required." They do a roaring trade, with smart tourists knowing Bangkok is best tackled by taking a valium in the morning and a viagra at night.

Along the edge of the road, people sit with newly-made friends at fold-up tables, drinking Chang, eating fried noodles, and making plans for the night. At least a few of them, though they don't yet know it, will wake in the morning with an ill-fitting three-piece suit, an offensive tattoo on their forehead, and a raging hard-on that won't go down.

CHACHOENGSAO

After a week of working, eating green curries, and waiting in traffic jams, I'm back at the Chinese embassy. I queue for a few hours to get back my passport and, yes, there it is inside: a Chinese tourist visa valid for twenty-five days from the date of entry.

After returning to the hostel and packing, I catch a mini-van to Chachoengsao, a town an hour north of Bangkok. In 2009, I spent a year teaching English at the university there, where I was paid £650 a month to teach half a dozen three-hour lessons a week. The university has two campuses, and it's an hour ride on a bus to one of them. I hated buses so much that I left the job despite it otherwise being a cushy gig. The irony of that now, when I spend more time on buses than bus drivers do.

Mae, a Filipino I worked with at the university, has set up a makeshift language centre in the back room of a shop. She's asked me to help out for a lesson, thinking the parents will be pleased to see a white face there. Teaching in Thailand is that superficial.

I have three years of teaching experience, but the last of those was over four years ago, and all of them were teaching twelve-to-twenty-one-year-olds. Today, I'm dealing with a room of four-year-olds. I don't like kids that little. They have a ten-second attention span and can pee their pants at any time.

The class starts with me sat on the floor, and the kids sat in a semi-circle around me. I've prepared a birds and the bees talk, but Mae hands me a sheet of questions to ask them instead: "What's your name? Where do you come from? How many people in your family? etc." The kids can answer all of them, though in a robotic, Dalek-like voice, which makes me think they don't know what they're saying: "Name Pui. Four-year-old. Five people family. Exterminate, exterminate."

Next, picture cards are spread on the floor for a game of match the rhyming words. The rules are complex, but I'll do my best to explain: I say a word on one of the cards and they have to pick up not only the card with the word on it but also a card with a word that rhymes with the first word. They go nuts for the game. So much so that I decide I'll sell the format to the BBC for a million pounds, for use on Saturday night TV.

Then the worst case scenario happens: one of the girls starts crying. Men get locked up for years for finding themselves in a situation like this. I look on the floor for pee but there's none. My repertoire of funny faces helps none one bit. I resort to calling in reinforcements. Mae strokes her head for thirty seconds and she stops crying and starts laughing. I thank Mae for saving me from a ten-year stretch in the Bangkok Hilton.

Next, Mae plays some videos so the kids can sing and dance. "Come on, Mark," she says, "we have to show them what to do. You sing and I'll dance. Three, two, one." I live out my rockstar dreams, singing, Sex Pistols-style, classics like *Heads, Shoulders, Knees, and Toes* and *I'm A Jelly Bear, I'm A Gummy Bear*. I've never seen four-year-olds mosh so hard.

The class finishes with me pointing at picture cards on a board, and the children repeating the words after me. I test each of them, one-on-one, on all fifteen images, which depict words ending in "all". When you say fall, ball, and tall fifty-plus times each in ten minutes, they stop sounding like real words, and you start to question both your sanity and whether the English language is little more than a fragile sham that could collapse at any time.

After the last kid has left, and I've done a final check for puddles, I fall into a chair feeling frazzled. There's no way I could do that all day every day. If I somehow find myself with a kid of my own, the little sod will be off to boarding school as soon as he can walk.

From here, I'm heading to the province of Maha

Sarakham, in the north of Thailand, 450 km from Chachoengsao. I'm going with Ben - someone else I worked with at the uni - and Pear, his Thai wife, to spend Songkran there, the Thai New Year holiday.

MAHA SARAKHAM

The village we're staying in, where Pear grew up, is small and rural. It consists of a crossroad and a dozen wooden houses. Locals welcome us as we get out the car, greeting us with hugs and handshakes. One man shakes my hand, then grabs my balls with his other hand. He does the same to Ben, which makes me feel better. A sexual assault shared is a sexual assault halved.

Cobwebs and dust fill every nook and cranny of Pear's family's house. Pear says her Mum is too old to clean the house properly - an excuse I've been using for years - and sets about cleaning it herself. Ben and I should help, but it's against Thai culture for men to do chores, and after an overnight road-trip without sleep, I've not got the enthusiasm to champion the feminist cause. We instead skulk off to drink Sang Som, a Thai rum distilled from sugarcane.

Chicken is for lunch, but we have to catch it first. The dozens running around sense they're on the menu and scarper every which way. We set off in pursuit.

Me: "Get that one."

Ben: "Which one? They all look the same."

Me: "The fat one. It'll be slowest."

Pear's Uncle: "Gaiiiiiiiiiiiiiiiiiiiiiiiii."

Me: "What did he say?"

Ben: "Chickeeeeeeeeeeeeeeeen."

Me: "Fair enough. Gaiiiiiiiiiiiiiiiiiiiiiii."

After dashing around fields for ten minutes, we finally corner and catch one. Held by the neck, it's taken into a shed. It reappears forty-five minutes later in the form of tasty grilled pieces, which we eat with rice, sat under a mango tree.

A middle-aged woman, who's joined us for a chicken wing, tells me, via Pear's translation, "I have two beautiful daughter. You want marry? You handsome foreigner. You rich. I want them marry you. You can choose which one like best. One seventeen-year-old, one eighteen-year-old."

Tempting as it is to marry a teenage country bumpkin, and spend the next decades chasing chickens around fields, I politely decline. Still, nice to have a Plan B.

After lunch - by which point Pear's uncle has been KO'd by too much Sang Som - we go to a lake to catch some fish. A local man tries to teach me to use an oval-shaped fishing net. I hurl it into the lake as far and as wide as I can, which turns out to be not very far and not very wide. I wait a minute, then wade into the water to gather the net and bring it back to the bank to tally my haul. After double and triple checking the numbers, my total number of fish is zero. Give me a fish, and you'll feed me for a day; give me a fishing net, and I'll starve.

The man tries it a couple of times himself and also doesn't catch anything, which I have mixed emotions about: I want to eat fish, but I don't want to be exposed as an incompetent fisherman. He goes away and comes back with a different style net, similar in size and shape to the type used on a badminton court. He and Ben each take an end of the net and stretch it out under the water, then plod up and down with it. It's not the most compelling viewing, so I challenge Pear and Ben's son to a mud-fight - which I lose. The blow of defeat is softened by seeing the others have caught a dozen fish.

By this point, I'm covered in sweat and mud. A shower would be refreshing, but there isn't one. There's no running water at the house, only a couple of containers of rainwater: one for drinking, one for washing. I use a bowl to scoop out water and pour it over myself. The same bowl is used for bot-bot cleaning. It's not easy, believe me.

Later, we grill the fish and eat it sat on the driveway of Pear's family's house. A guy turns up with a bucket of locusts he's collected from a field. He tips them into a pan, fries them alive, and shares them around, getting some fish in return. Swapping locusts for fish is a shrewd move. The fried locusts are crunchy on the outside, gooey on the inside. They don't taste too bad. Anything tastes okay if you fry it first and wash it down with alcohol.

As we eat, Pear talks about the work people in the village do: "People my family's village, many not have job, but some have land a little, so can farming. My family have land for farm rice. Normally it good, but now have problem with government about buy rice."

Ben explains that Thailand is the world's largest exporter of rice, and the Thai government sought to flex their power on the international market by hiking the price of Thai rice. However, the dimwits didn't factor in that buyers might baulk at paying inflated Thai prices when there are other rice-producing countries they could buy from. Which is what they did, leaving Thailand with an excess of rice. Instead of farmers getting more for their produce, as promised by the government, they're now struggling to sell it at all.

After eating, it's time for a water-fight. During Songkran, which comes at the hottest time of the year, Thailand turns into a water-fight battlefield. Everyone has the right to soak anyone. Super Soakers are the standard weapon of choice, but some prefer the grenade-type approach of using a bucket. We drive around nearby villages in Ben's car. Ben's drunk, but so are all the other drivers, which makes it fine. Groups of Thais, mainly eighteen-to-thirty years old, line the roads: chucking water, swigging Sang Som, and bopping to techno beats. I slyly drive-by shoot of them, poking my water gun out of a marginally wound down window and squirting the suckers in the face. This is more fun than Christmas, which people spend cooped-up in their house watching TV. For Songkran, you're outdoors in the sunshine, mixing with all and sundry. Plus, have you tried shooting someone with a Super Soaker on Christmas Day? It doesn't go down well.

After an evening spent drinking more Sang Som, I retire to my bed for the night: a mat in the corner of the living room. Cockroaches scurry across the floor; mosquitoes pester me. I'm too hot if I cover myself with a sheet for protection, but if I don't cover myself, I get bitten. I look for a cupboard I could sleep in. They're all too small.

I'm so tired that I fall asleep despite being feasted upon. But not for long: I'm woken by the sound of a crack coming from inside my mouth. I look in the mirror and see a chunk of a front tooth veneer - which I had fitted in Bangkok - has chipped off.

Screw you, Buddha. First my toe, now my tooth. When I see you in Nirvana, I'll shove a flip-flop up your arse.

LAOS

VIENTIANE

I reach the Laos border via an overnight bus from Bangkok.
Yes, Bangkok, not Maha Sarakham. I had to backtrack to
Bangkok to get my tooth fixed. Spending the next few
months, until I get back to Europe, resembling a broken-
toothed hillbilly wasn't an option. Neither was letting any
chump in a white coat stick a drill in my mouth.

"Mr Walter, now put drill your mouth."

"Argh! Stop! You're drilling through my tongue!"

"Very sorry, Mr Walter. Let try again."

"Motherfucker! You've gone through my cheek!"

"Sorry again, Mr Walter. Only work buffalo before. First
time work teeth man."

That's how I envisaged any visit to a dentist in Laos or
China playing out.

Vientiane, thirty minutes drive from the Thai-Laos
border, is so laid-back and sleepy that it's hard to believe it's

a capital city. The National Library and National Museum are both smaller than a Marks & Spencers in a provincial British town. There's not even a McDonald's.

Colonialism has influenced the architecture and layout; not the British to blame this time but the French, who ruled Laos from 1803 to 1953. They might have been better off sticking with the French because it's been a one-party socialist republic since 1975, run by the Lao People's Revolutionary Party. It's fair to say communism hasn't worked out for Laos. It's one of the poorest countries in the world. A third of the population live below the international poverty line, on less than £1 per day.

With that in mind, you might expect Vientiane to be super cheap. Yet it's not. Goods cost 20-30% more than similar ones in Bangkok due to Laos not having the land, resources, and infrastructure to produce much themselves, meaning they have to truck and fly most items in from Thailand, Vietnam, and China. Still, money does go a long way here, and because £1 is equal to 13,500 kip - the local currency - when I take £150 out of the ATM I become a millionaire. I knew I would be one day.

Outside the bus station, women wearing wicker hats sell fresh produce like honeycomb, bamboo, and ginger. Others march about with poles over their shoulders, a heavy load of wares stored in dozens of buckets balanced on either end. One man sits beside a stack of chickens piled on top of each other; their feet tied together to prevent escape. Having chased chickens in Thailand, I understand taking extreme measures not to let them escape, having gotten hold of them. Another man has adopted a specialist approach, selling a single rhino horn. I don't know what use anyone would have for it - other than sticking it on their head and pretending to be a rhino, which I imagine would be fun for only a short time.

Only one person asks me for money: a shaggy-looking Australian. "Mate," he says, "I've got no money. Can you give me £1 to buy a sandwich?"

"You've not even got £1?

"Nah, mate. I was waiting for some money to get transferred, but it hasn't come through. So can I have £1?"

"I'm not an on-demand sandwich funding service."

"Fuck off."

The city's principal landmark is a concrete Arc De Triomphe lookalike called Patuxai. It was built to commemorate those who fought for independence from France. If there's logic in making a smaller, crappier version of a monument from a country you've defeated, I can't see it. A sign on the monument describes it as a "monster of concrete". Possibly this came out of Google Translate wrong. It's not, however, far off the mark.

As I walk, I get some stares from locals, which I return with a nod and a smile. Each time, I get a smile back. I even smile at the school girl on a motorcycle who speeds around a corner on the pavement. She would have hit me had I not leapt out the way. I'm within my rights to throw a stone at her as she races off without apologising, but if locals see me chucking stones at school girls, it will cancel out the diplomatic smiling work I've been doing.

I pass through Anovong Park, adjacent to the mighty Mekong River, which flows through Laos for 1,500 km of its course. In the park is a statue of Chao Anouvong, the last King of Laos, with a sword by his side and an open hand outstretched. This friendly approach, while admirable, has been Laos's downfall. They've been invaded and ruled by several countries. The size of their army isn't much of a deterrent: thirty-thousand soldiers. I could round up thirty-thousand and one in an hour on Facebook.

Along the riverfront promenade, middle-aged women do aerobic exercises to techno tunes warbling from battered speakers. Near them, a man with an open parachute on his back runs up and down, trying to catch some wind. I'm not sure if he's testing it for holes or he's landed in the wrong place and is trying to take off again.

While I'm sat on a bench on the promenade, a woman on a bicycle rides up to me. "Pedicure?" she asks. "I see feet you. Not beautiful."

"Did you say pedicure?" I ask, thinking I must have misheard, as it would be odd for her to ask me that.

She points to the front basket of her bicycle, which is filled with pedicure paraphernalia, and says, "I give pedicure. £1.50."

"Here? Now?"

"Yes."

My feet do look manky. More so than usual because yesterday the nail on my big toe fell off, after slowing dying since I hit it on the rock in the car park at the chicken temple in Bangkok.

"You can't polish a turd," I tell her.

"I not understand. You want pedicure?"

"No, thank you."

The nail on my other big toe fell off a few years ago after I banged it playing football, and it's never properly recovered. With a couple of skanky big toes, I'll never fulfil my dream of being a flip-flop model.

LUANG PRABANG

Last night I arrived in Luang Prabang, a misty city of temples in northern Laos, after a day-long bus ride through a precipitous jungled-landscape, on a barrier-less, potholed road - the country's main highway - that meandered through clusters of wooden houses and wicker shacks. Pigs, goats, and chickens roamed roadside - even a few elephants too.

Today, I'm up at 5.30 am to watch the alms-giving ceremony that takes place every morning in Luang Prabang. Monks from each of the city's temples - and there are a lot of temples - stream the streets in single file lines. At one point, a hundred-plus walk past in one line. Such a sight gives unholy thoughts to anyone who played the original Grand Theft Auto, where mowing down lines of monks would boost your score. Locals sit or crouch at the side of the road, their heads lower than the monks' as a sign of respect. They give each monk who passes some food, like a portion of rice or some vegetables, which they place into the basket each monk carries. Monks aren't allowed to use money, and so rely on this ceremony to get their grub. Locals give it to get some Karma points. The more a person racks up in their lifetime, the better the life they'll have when they're reborn. Accumulate too few points, and life as a dung beetle awaits.

Despite it being so early, the streets are busy because, as well as monks and locals, tourists have risen to witness the spectacle. Signs state it's a sacred ritual, not a gimmick for tourists, and not to get close to the monks or use flash photography. Ignoring this request, some stand within a metre of the monks, and blind them with flashes. I hope they enjoy looking at those photos when they get home. They've paid a high price for them: being face first in dung for eternity. I take a photo too but while sitting on the kerb on the other side of the street. Anyway, Buddha already hates me, so it doesn't matter if I take a photo of a monk, or steal a tuk-tuk and mow down a hundred of them.

Later, I cross the murky, brown Mekong on a rickety bamboo bridge and follow paths past small shacks. Near one, a teenager is high up a coconut tree using a stick to poke at the bounty on offer, for free to anyone brave enough. Below him, two friends position themselves, hoping the delivery falls into their hands, not onto their heads.

I walk along a path, through some trees, and come out in a clearing beside a house on the riverfront. An old man approaches from a boat on the bank. "You speak French?" he asks me.

"No, only English."

"I speak French good. English just bit."

"Is that your boat?"

"Yes. Also that one. And that one too."

"And this is your house?"

"This house number four."

"Where are the other three?"

"One over here. Two in the town."

"Cool."

"You buy me beer?"

"No."

A man with three boats and four houses can buy his own beer. If anything, he should buy me one.

After lunch, I go to Kuang Si Waterfalls, part of a nearby national park. The main waterfall is a three-tier, sixty-metre cascade of water, falling over rocks coated in algae and moss. I've not seen many waterfalls, but this is the best of them. I attempt the steep hike to the top, but soon give up. Climbing a muddy, twisting path in flip-flops is a fool's errand. A fool I might be, but an errand-running one I'm not. Flip-flops, great as they are, aren't suitable for some activities, and this is one, along with skiing and scuba diving.

Instead, I spend hours lazing in the jungle-shaded, multi-levelled, turquoise pools at the foot of the waterfall. Unseen objects move below the surface. To relax you need to persuade yourself that the odd-feeling thing brushing your thigh is a leaf or fish, not a leech or snake. I chat with people from around the world, including a Japanese finance worker, a South Korean restaurant owner, and a Vietnamese software programmer. We discuss topics ranging from the best age to get married (forty), to should Japan be allowed an army again (no), to whether or not bicycles in the Netherlands have brakes (not sure).

Back in Luang Prabang, I visit Wat Xieng Thong, an ornately decorated, gold-gilded temple. In the courtyard is an outdoor shrine under a gazebo. Candles burn among bouquets of flowers. People kneel to pray and present offerings. Music plays from speakers, and sounds, to my musically untrained ears, like xylophones, bongos, and flutes. It's not unlike the £3 *Summer Sunset On The Beach* CDs you find in supermarkets, which a cheapskate relative buys you for Christmas.

The monks of the temple are young, averaging twenty-to-twenty-five years old. Some, though, are mere boys. Becoming a monk means they get a good education and also Karma points for their whole family. They live for free in a scenic setting under sunny skies and don't have to worry about work or money. It sounds better than a life of doing a job you hate to pay for things you don't need.

Afterwards, I climb the steps to Phou Si Stupa, a temple on a hill in the centre of the city. On the way up is a woman stood behind a table of small cages, two birds in each one. People buy the birds from her so they can get Karma points for setting them free. I wonder how many Karma points I'd get for putting her in a cage. At the top of the hill, I see the sun setting over the dense jungle which surrounds Luang Prabang for as far as the eye can see. Looking around, I wonder what the Americans were trying to bomb here in the Vietnam War, during which they made Laos the world's most heavily bombed country, per capita, in history. The plus-sized burger-munchers dropped 270 million "bombies" (bombs, cluster bombs, and the bombs within cluster bombs) on Laos, a quarter of which failed to detonate. These are called UXO (unexploded ordnance). Clearance work has yet to be completed, meaning much of Laos is like a minefield. More than twenty thousand have been killed or injured by UXOs since the end of the war in 1973. Of those, thirteen thousand lost a limb.

On the way back to my room, I stop off to buy a £35 bus ticket to take me to Kunming in China, a twenty-four-hour bus ride away. The prospect of that tortuous journey is worsened when at my room I read an article on the BBC News website about a terrorist attack earlier today at the train station in Urumqi, capital of Xinjiang.

> "Deadly Terrorist Attack At Xinjiang Railway Station: A bomb and knife attack at a railway station in China's western Xinjiang region has killed three and injured seventy-nine others. The attackers used knives to stab people at the station exit and detonated explosives at the same time."

There's a link within the article to another one about a terrorist attack last month at Kunming train station, where I'm heading tomorrow. But there's no point worrying about getting stabbed or blown up until I'm in the country, which isn't a certainty. Because I was bored of waiting in embassy queues, and because it's not my preferred route, I didn't apply for the Mongolian visa the Chinese embassy told me to get. It's a valid reason for turning me away at the Laos-China border. Hopefully, they won't give a toss, or I can bribe them, but it'll be a nervous twelve-hour ride to the border to find out.

CHINA

KUNMING

I'm on the sleeper bus - it has beds instead of seats - from Luang Prabang to Kunming. Not that I've had much sleep. The suspension is a shambles and stretches of the journey have been along unpaved, rocky roads. But I don't care that I've only had an hour of sleep. And I don't care that my level of dishevelment puts me so far into scarecrow territory I can no longer see the border with dignity. All I care about is that I've damn well made it into China.

Anxiety about my visa progressively intensified during the twelve hours from Luang Prabang to the border town of Mohan, reaching a sweaty, panicked, dry-mouthed conclusion in the queue in the immigration building. But the worries were unnecessary. The border officials didn't ask a single question. They even smiled at me. With that obstacle negotiated, I can start fretting about China problem number two: terrorist attacks.

I arrive in chilly, overcast Kunming after twenty-six hours on the bus. I'm sharing a room at a hostel - which is smart and modern, and similar to some I stayed at in Australia - with seven others, who are all Chinese. "I read Englishman like talk about weather," one of them tells me, "and social status, up, middle, and down is very important. My favourite English figure is Mr Bean. Susan Boyle sing nice, but I don't like her face."

Walking the streets, I get more than a few stares and double-takes. It could be because I'm a foreigner, or it could be because I'm walking around in flip-flops and a bright, stripy jumper. The locals seem to have come to a consensus only to wear clothing that's grey, brown, or black.

From a food cart, I buy a pot of roast potatoes coated in spicy herbs. I hovered to see what others were paying, then blurted my best "ni hao" (Chinese for "hello") and pointed at what I wanted. The seller asked me something, to which I replied with a nod despite having no idea what the question was. I thought this better than saying, "Sorry, I don't understand." Speaking in your own language, even a few words, is a mistake. It results in an exchange that sounds like one between Siri and a Furby.

There's not a word of English anywhere. I should learn more Chinese, but it's tough. It took me an hour just to learn "ni hao". The language is comprised of thousands of intricate symbols. You need to learn at least 2,500 of them to be able to read a newspaper. Unfortunately, the symbols don't depict the words. The symbol for "cat" isn't a small image of a cat, which would simplify learning the language. Another complication is there being several regional languages in addition to Mandarin, the official language. People use their regional language for everyday communication, and each of those is unintelligible to speakers of the others. But despite the regional differences and multitude of symbols, the consensus of international language experts is that English, with its subtleties, inconsistencies, and extensive vocabulary, is harder to learn than Chinese. So if the Chinese can learn English, I should be able to learn Chinese.

While their language might be better than English, when it comes to toilets, the West wins. Inside a toilet block at a market are half a dozen waist-high, door-less cubicles. A single trench runs beneath them, over which people squat and drop. You would think the dumpers would want the ordeal to be over ASAP, but no one is in a rush; they're chatting, smoking, and reading newspapers - all mid-squat. They should pay more attention to the task at hand. As much brown matter ends up on the floor as in the trench. There's no toilet paper, water bucket, or hosepipe. I dread to think how they're wiping clean. I'm not hanging about to find out.

In Kunming's central square, surly police officers patrol with metre-long metal poles in hand. For hitting people, I assume, not for impromptu pole-vaulting. Children holding fishing rods stand around a fountain filled with thousands of goldfish, trying to catch either dinner or a pet. Blind men and women in white coats give head and shoulder massages, but not toe ones, to people seated on plastic chairs. A guy with no arms sits on the floor with a paintbrush held between his toes, drawing intricate Chinese characters on the pavement.

Near the central square is Green Lake, so called because

the water is green and topped with lily pads, and leafy trees line its walkways and islands. At a corner of the lake, I see what I think is a Shaolin monk. A crowd has gathered to watch him. He somersaults and air punches, then crouches to pummel bricks with the palms of his hands. He then swigs from a wrapped bottle and roars. Next, he takes three metal rods and bends them around his neck. After a couple of minutes, they're so tightly wrapped that he's gasping for air. Then he sits and meditates.

In the evening, I go to reception at the hostel, where they offer a travel agency service. I tell them I'd like a train ticket to Chengdu.

"It take twenty hour for go Kunming. You can hard seater, hard sleeper, or soft sleeper."

"What's the difference between the three?"

"Hard seater, just seat. Many people hard seater. No much space. Hard sleeper, you get bed. Same like bunk bed. One section train have one hundred bed. Soft sleeper, you get bed more nice. Four bed in private train section."

"Soft sleeper, please. I don't care what it costs."

The cost is £38. I would have paid three times as much to spend twenty hours with only three Chinese people spitting, smoking, and shouting, instead of ninety-nine of the buggers doing it.

KUNMING TO CHENGDU

At the entrance to Kunming train station, my bag gets scanned, and I'm patted down. Thousands of people loiter inside. The only white face is mine. It's the easiest ever game of *Where's Wally?*. Police patrol with poles, soldiers stand with guns. It's as safe as it can be, but I take an extra measure: standing in a corner with my arms aloft and one knee raised - à la *Karate Kid* - until it's time to board the train. The cabin has four beds - two below, two on top - and there's a sheet, duvet, and pillow on each. I have it to myself, for now at least.

The journey is through sprawling agricultural expanses. It's not super-sized fields for super-sized farming, but thousands of tiered plots, each no more than ten square metres. Bent over workers, planting and ploughing, take the place of machinery, making the land look like the world's largest allotment. Hundreds of grotty mines, plants, and factories blemish the beauty, pumping black fumes into the grey air. The price to be paid for being the workhouse of the world.

In the afternoon, three Chinese guys, twenty-to-thirty years old, join me in the cabin. The two on the top bunks, who appear to be mates, peer down at me, gawking like I'm an alien. They've likely never been in close quarters with a foreigner before. One of them - let's call him Chinaman One - gets out his phone and indicates he wants to take a photo of me. I nod to say it's ok and flash a cheesy smile. He snaps the photo, says "khank o" - an attempt at "thank you" - and looks pleased with himself, having captured a once in a lifetime shot of a white man in the wild.

Later, Chinaman One waves a 100 yuan note at me. I work out that he wants to know if I have any foreign currency. He wants to do an exchange, but I give him a one dollar note and some Thai coins for free. Within five minutes of this, Chinaman One and his pal - Chinaman

Two - have left their beds and are down on mine, sitting either side of me. I use Google Maps on Chinaman One's phone to show them where I'm from, and they pore over my passport, carefully turning the pages like it's the world's oldest book. Chinaman Two admires my beard, while Chinaman One takes great pride in showing me his tattoos. At one point, Chinaman Two goes to the restaurant carriage to buy beers, beef jerky, and chicken knees for us to share. After eating, the three of us pose for photos with each other. Then Chinaman One types out "I love you" on his phone and hands it to me. He's fast-tracking the relationship. He might propose before we arrive in Chengdu.

There's another photo session while smoking with them at the end of the carriage. A ticket inspector walks past and wants in on the action too. Between them, they manage to ask, "China good? China Bad?"

"China good," I say. I'm not saying it to be polite, either. So far China has been good, and not one of the locals has tried to kill me.

I've had a great time with these guys. The differences between us are more superficial than they are substantial. If you take the time to try to get to know people, I think that's true for everyone, everywhere.

CHENGDU

I'm staying at a £6 a night hostel nestled within a district of dated flats, accessed by passing through side streets too narrow to fit a car down. Around the neighbourhood, people sit outside shops and on street corners, smoking, drinking tea, and playing Mahjong, a traditional Chinese game played with tiles. They smoke, gamble, move tiles, smoke, sip tea, spit, smoke, and move more tiles. Others, on bicycles and mopeds, work their way around the market stalls lining the streets, stopping to pick up produce to place in their front basket.

I assess the options for breakfast. I decide against intestine soup or the tail of something - or a frog, one of which leaps from a bowl and attempts a getaway, but is spotted by the seller and scooped from the mucky floor and chucked back into the bowl. I opt for fried sticky rice, a doughnut-type thing, and a hot bun with a meat filling. While tasty and cheap, Chinese street food isn't the healthiest and is probably one of the reasons - along with smoking like chimneys - that the average life expectancy in China is five-plus years lower than in many Western countries.

In Tianfu Square, in the city centre, is a white statue of Mao Tse-Tung, the founding father of modern China, who died in 1976. Those who love him say he revolutionised the country, putting it on the path to power. Those who hate him say his policies killed millions - sometimes accidentally, sometimes on purpose - and he destroyed much of China's cultural heritage.

While I'm stood deciding whether or not to throw eggs at the Mao statue, a man approaches and says, "Today birthday my girlfriend. You sing happy birthday?"

"Err, ok. Where is she?"

"She not here."

He points to his camera.

"On video?" I ask.

"Yes."

"What's her name?"

He says something longer than two syllables that I forget before he's even finished saying it, then "Four, two, one."

"Happy birthday to you, happy birthday to you, happy birthday dear Chinawoman, happy birthday to you."

Near Tianfu Square is Chunxi, a shopping district with long, wide streets of clothes stores. H&M, Zara, Rolex, Armani, and Calvin Klein are just some of the international brands making an appearance. I thought there would be something in the communist handbook banning the sale of undies for £20 a pair. Hordes of people are shopping, spunking yuan all over. So you can stop shedding tears, as I know you do, for Chinese people slaving in sweatshops, doing eighteen-hour shifts, seven days a week. They're not sat in rags, eating plain noodles, looking longingly through glossy brochures of Europe and America.

From what I've seen, Chengdu is better than Birmingham, Manchester, and Liverpool, the largest English cities after London. There are fewer boarded-up shops, homeless people, and old cars; more designer stores and impressive buildings; and public transport is in better condition and cheaper. Countries in the West need to pull their heads out the sand. They're getting left behind. If it carries on as it is, in fifty years Westerners might find themselves sat in rags, eating plain bread, looking longingly through glossy brochures of China.

I take the metro to People's Park, which is packed even though it's 11 am on Monday. Some are strolling, others - mostly old-timers - partake in activities like dancing and tai chi - even kung fu. Chinese pensioners are an active bunch. I've seen loads of them pumping iron in the exercise yards common in Chinese neighbourhoods. I wonder what type of herbs they're putting in their tea, and how legal they are.

In the middle of the park is a traditional teahouse, with a few dozen people sat on chairs outside. I take a seat and order a tea for £1, hoping I've chosen one of those that power grannies to bench press and roundhouse kick. As I sip the tea, a man with a flashlight on his head, and an odd-looking metal utensil in his hand, shows me a card that says in English that he provides an ear-cleaning service for £2. My ears could do with a clean, having accumulated months of filth, and possibly an insect or two. But is a teahouse the right time and place? No, it's not. What is it with Asians doing what should be private - ear-cleaning, pedicures, and shitting - in front of others? I tell him no thanks, but someone nearby takes him up on his offer. He does a thorough job. Perhaps too thorough: the utensil is so far into the woman's ear it's verging on poking out the other.

Continuing around the park, I come across hundreds of lonely hearts ads on laminated A4 paper attached to bamboo poles stuck in the ground and hung from string tied between trees. One has an English translation.

"Local Unmarried Girl

Was born on September 28, 1985. 1.66 metres tall. Bachelor's degree. She is a veteran working in the state's financial department (Chengdu) in Sichuan. She has good looks, elegant temperament, good family upbringing.

Will Be Marry With

The one should be born in 1976-1985, with the height

over 1.75 m and outstanding ability. And have the sense of responsibility and good family upbringing. Good health, no bad habits, and who is willing to live with family."

A woman taps my arm, points at the ad, pulls a photo album from her bag, and motions that I should look at it. She's much older than the 1985 date of birth in the ad, so I assume it's for her daughter. I browse the album, containing about twenty photos, giving a thumbs-up or saying "beautiful" on every other page. In truth, though, we're talking 4/10 - at best. She didn't mention that in the ad. Still, maybe I'll give her a go. I'm thirty-one and unmarried. The clock is ticking. I recheck her list of requirements to see if I make the grade. Born between 1976-1985? Yes. Taller than 1.75 metres? Yes. Outstanding ability? Yes. Sense of responsibility? No. I point at that line on the ad and make a pained expression to indicate I'm not up to scratch.

Later, I visit the Chengdu Research Base of Giant Panda Breeding, home to the largest number of captive giant pandas in the world. It's like a zoo that only has pandas in it. There are no bars or cages, though; the pandas have large, leafy enclosures built into what would be their natural habitat. Giant pandas need places like this because they're an endangered species. There are few of them left: two thousand in the wild and three hundred in captivity. This site began in 1987 with six giant pandas, but now has more than eighty - a result of rescues and romances. They re-introduce pandas into the wild where possible and also rent them to other zoos to raise funds. Panda pimping is ethically dubious, but at least they're doing it for a good cause. There are a few baby pandas, looking cute with their fluffy fur and black eyes. For £190 you can hold one and have your photo taken with it. For that price, I'd expect not only to hold it and snap a photo but to have it barbecued and served on a plate. At one point, I pass a line of hundred-plus school kids, being looked after not by teachers but by soldiers. A couple of the children shriek "hello" at me as I walk by, to which I respond likewise, though with less volume. My reply sets them off like falling dominoes, one by one squealing at me until I've passed them all. Signs say to keep quiet, but keeping a hundred-plus six-year-olds quiet, when to their left is a foreigner and to their right are pandas pooping, is a task beyond the whole Chinese army.

Back at the hostel, I chat to the owner, Susu, who speaks near-perfect English. I need to book my next train ticket, so it's crunch time on whether to head north-west through Xinjiang to Kazakhstan or to go north-east to Mongolia, via Beijing. "You can go to Xinjiang, even though it's dangerous," she says. "The separatists risk losing international support if foreigners get hurt." It's not a ringing endorsement, but I'll roll with it. A decision that hopefully won't roll me into an early grave.

Susu takes me to a travel agency to buy a ticket for the train to Urumqi, the capital of Xinjiang. The travel agent says, via Susu, that flying from Chengdu to Urumqi costs only £20 more than taking the train, and that flying takes four hours, whereas the train takes forty-eight. Susu tells me I'm a fool for taking the train, and I think I'm a fool for taking the train, but I buy the £80 train ticket anyway.

Using the internet in the evening, several times I forget Facebook is blocked and try to load the site. There's no message to say it's blocked; it just won't load. The Chinese aren't having their human rights abused, though, by being denied photos of cute cats. They have the world's largest online community, with hundreds of millions using the internet for social purposes. They use Chinese alternatives to Facebook and Twitter, like Qzone and Sina Weibo. The government permit usage of those social networks because, unlike the Western ones, they can get full access to the data as and when they want, without explanation. The Chinese government also has thousands of cyber police whose job it is to monitor websites and social networks. They use a filtering system to sort through the billions of posts made each day, that searches for combinations of keywords deemed politically or socially sensitive. For example: "Chinese soldiers. Unarmed students. Tiananmen Square." If someone posts a criticism of the government, it'll be quickly deleted. Do it repeatedly, and they'll get a midnight knock on their door and not be seen again for a while.

The cyber police haven't censored articles about the latest terrorist incident, which happened yesterday. The attack, in Guangzhou, again took place at a train station. It's being pinned on the Muslim separatist movement in Xinjiang. I wonder, though, with all the attacks occurring at train stations, if bus drivers are to blame, annoyed at people taking trains instead of buses. The terrorists went easy this time, sticking to stabbing people, instead of stabbing and bombing them; but the kicker for me is a Westerner was one of those attacked, which didn't happen with previous incidents. That's now three terrorist attacks at train stations in the last seven weeks, with thirty-five killed and two-hundred-plus injured. And tomorrow I'm taking a train to the capital of the province responsible for the attacks.

URUMQI

I'm nearing the end of my forty-eight-hour train ride from Chengdu to Urumqi, on which I've traversed rural land, lunar-like expanses, and snow-covered mountain ranges. Much of the terrain looked inhospitable, but unlike the Australian Outback, where there were massive distances between signs of life, here there's always some settlement or structure in sight. I haven't had a shower (there are none onboard), and I haven't changed my clothes (no one else has), but I've slept well and feel good. I'd happily spend forty-eight hours more on here because being on here means I'm not yet where I'm headed, and fuck knows what's waiting for me there. I've no right to be in this part of China. There's a definite chance the police or army, who will be in numbers at Urumqi train station, won't take kindly to me being there. Being locked up and then deported isn't a remote possibility.

The train arrives at Urumqi a couple of minutes ahead of schedule - an impressive achievement for a forty-eight-hour trip. A half-hour train ride in the UK somehow always manages to arrive late. Dozens of police line the platform, directing people towards one exit. They yell at anyone dawdling. I attract stares from them but none approach. Outside, rows of bulletproof vest-wearing soldiers, with automatic guns and riot shields, form a cordon around the entrance. On the other side of the cordon stands a crowd of scruffy, irate men, sporting moustaches and wearing ill-fitting suits. They shout and wave clenched fists in the air. I make a beeline for the exit gap in the cordon, and the bus stop a couple of metres beyond it. There's a bus about to depart. I've no idea where it's going but I board it, reasoning anywhere is better than here.

I get off the bus after ten minutes at somewhere central-looking and wander around trying to orientate myself - difficult when the street signs are in Chinese. Via a long walk, a taxi ride, and another long walk, I find the hotel I pre-booked: Yijia Chain Hotel Lijing Boutique Hotel. It's the first hotel I've come across that has the word "Hotel" twice in its name. The Chinese haven't gotten to grips with naming things. Somewhere in China will be a place called Hotel Hotel Hotel.

Half the people in Urumqi don't look Chinese at all. They look more like Borat-does-Islam than the guy you buy chow mien from. They give me long, dodgy looks, as do the soldiers stood on street corners, flanked by tanks - turrets manned and primed to shoot. I should stay indoors as much I can. It's risky being here at all and there's no point taking further risks by swanning around for the sake of it. I'll need to be out and about a bit, though, to get a visa for Kazakhstan. Like China, they're stingy with their visas and don't hand them out willy-nilly to the likes of me.

After two hours of searching for the Kazakhstan consulate, I turn a corner and see a throng, of a hundred or more, trying to force their way into a couple of dreary buildings in a manner that makes Black Friday shoppers look like pensioners at the post office. This must be the place. When a guard emerges from one of the doors, people surge at him, waving their paperwork and making their plea. A few are let in; the rest are left to wait. In the space between the buildings is a noticeboard, but none of the notices are in English, so I'm not sure which door I need to "queue" at. I make a guess and join the scrum.

After thirty minutes of elbow jabbing and shoulder barging, during which I make little progress, I see that two white faces have appeared in the crowd at the other door. I walk over to them, hoping they can shed some light on the situation. Tash says this is the building for foreigners to apply for a visa. Her friend Callum is a giant of a man and is towards the front of the mob, making full use of his height and weight advantage. Tash shouts encouragement: "Come on, Callum. Push them out the way. You're bigger than them." Twenty minutes later, a guard comes out and says, according to Callum's translation, to leave and come back tomorrow.

At the hotel, I feel ill and start to sneeze. I go to a pharmacy, but language confusion means I leave with nothing. I make do with a can of Red Bull from a street stall. Rather than making me feel better, it only makes me sneeze faster. I spend the night speed sneezing, watching Fashion TV (the only English-speaking channel out of about seven hundred), and researching why Xinjiang is a battleground reaching boiling point.

To summarise: Xinjiang is home to an ethnic group called Uighurs, whose language, religion, and customs are closely aligned with Turkic countries like Kazakhstan, Afghanistan, Kyrgyzstan, Tajikistan, and Pakistan. The

Uighurs have from time to time had their own homeland, independent from China; most recently from 1944-1949, when Xinjiang was a country called Second East Turkestan Republic. China seized back the land in 1949. They took Tibet a year later. Both Xinjiang and Tibet want to be independent, but China won't give up the two mineral-rich provinces. The Uighurs and Tibetans can't force out the Chinese, but neither will they submit to them, resulting in a strained stalemate. The Tibetans are using diplomacy to try to gain independence, whereas the Uighurs favour a more radical approach: stabbing and bombing people. Both methods have their merits but have proved equally ineffective, with neither country being any closer to independence now than they were sixty years ago.

I also learn that Urumqi is 2,500+ km from the nearest coastline, making it further from the sea than any other city in the world. So while terrorist attacks might be a problem, tsunamis won't be.

I'm back at the Kazakhstan consulate, confronted by a rabble as large and rowdy as yesterday. But with Callum psyched-up like a man possessed, we get inside within an hour. It transpires, however, that in this building we can only fill in the visa form and get it reviewed. The application has to be submitted in the other building.

The other door doesn't have a guard outside it but is enclosed in a cage. The cage isn't locked, but the cage door can only be opened from the inside. Some people enter the cage as others exit from it and go inside the building. Four times out of five they get kicked out seconds later, but sometimes they manage to stay inside, which encourages others to try their luck. After an hour, we join one such raid on the door with three Uzbekistanis. We make it inside, but a guard chucks us out. A minute later, the door opens, and the guard lets the three Uzbekistanis in but blocks us. "Fuck you. You're a cunt," shouts Callum in his impenetrable Glaswegian accent. If the guard had understood what he said, the outburst would have earned us an extra week of waiting time.

Over the next ninety minutes, we make three more raids on the door. Each time, we get kicked out again. Eventually, we're let in and submit our application. But it's not yet job done. "Come back 22nd. You get visa then," the clerk tells me.

"That's nine days away. I can't wait that long."

"Come back 22nd. You get visa then."

"Can I pay more to get it in a few days?"

"Come back 22nd. You get visa then."

This means nine more days in Urumqi, trying not to get killed. And I have only eleven days left on my Chinese visa. If I come back in nine days and they tell me I can't have a visa, or I need to wait longer for it, I'll have no choice but to fly out of China.

Walking out, feeling sorry for myself, I scan the scrums and note the anguish on the faces of the people, many of whom were here yesterday. As frustrating as my experience here has been, I think as a foreigner I got preferential treatment. These poor sods could be coming back for days, or even weeks. And they have a good reason for wanting to go to Kazakhstan: to apply for asylum to escape persecution. Whereas Callum, Tash, and I are just going there on a jolly.

Even though my visa isn't confirmed, I decide to buy a ticket for the bus to Kazakhstan because if I wait until I get the visa, the bus might already be fully booked. A barbed wire perimeter surrounds the bus station. There are a couple of tanks, and even more soldiers than there were at the train station. Cars are searched, people are scanned, everyone must show ID. When a soldier puts his hand out for my ID, I reach for my pocket but then remember my passport is at the Kazakhstan consulate. I have no other ID.

"No-e speak-e Chinese-e. Me-e English-e. Me-e no-e ID-e," I say, thinking that adding an "e" to the end of words will somehow make them comprehensible to him.

He looks at me, expressionless, with his hand still outstretched.

I point to my flip-flops and repeat what I said before, but this time trying a new tactic: "No-a speak-a Chinese-a. Me-a English-a. Me-a no-a ID-a."

He waves me past, probably thinking I'm too mentally disabled to be a terrorist.

There's more confusion inside: the timetables and ticket counter signage are in Chinese and Uighur. I'm yet to learn my first Chinese character. I've been too busy watching Fashion TV. I join one of the queues, get to the front, and hand over a piece of paper stating my destination - Almaty - and departure date. The ticket clerk looks at it, then stares blankly at me. I say Almaty in as many ways and tones as I can think of. One of them - number twenty-three, I think -

hits home. "No, you...," she says, and points at the exit, twisting her hand to the right.

Outside, I wander around saying, "Bus. Almaty. Ticket," to anyone who'll listen, which isn't many. It's not a good spot to be dilly-dallying. Soldiers keep a keen eye on me, including one manning a tank turret. He's not likely to blast me to smithereens, but he might do if he's bored or thinks he'll get a medal. Through hand gestures and piecing together the odd word of broken English, I work out this isn't even the right bus station. This one is for domestic buses; there's another, down the road, for international ones.

At the right station, I buy a £45 ticket for the twenty-four-hour sleeper bus to Kazakhstan. I'm supposed to collect my visa in nine days time at 3 pm, and the bus departs at 6 pm. I'm cutting it fine but want to get moving ASAP. There's just one bus per day. If I wait until the day after, with then only a day left on my Chinese visa, a break-down or cancellation will force me to fly.

I check out of my hotel at midday and get to the Kazakhstan consulate, bag in tow, at 1 pm - two hours before the collection time for the visa. I'm cold and wet when I arrive and have to wait in the rain, without any cover. Tash and Callum aren't here today because they don't need their visa as urgently as I do. But I'm not alone in a mob of moustaches. With me are Jared and Kate, a couple from New Zealand, on a cycling tour of Asia.

"It's terrible what happened this morning, all those people being killed," says Jared, to which I look confused. "At the morning market by Renmin Park," he says, "two cars drove along the street throwing explosives out the window. More than thirty people were killed. It's been all over the news."

That park is only a kilometre from the hotel I've been staying at. I was there yesterday.

Jared's got more bad news: "We came here yesterday to collect our visas, which was the date they told us to come when we submitted our documents, but the guards came outside and shooed everyone away."

If that happens again today, I'm screwed.

At 4.15 pm, fifteen minutes before the consulate closes for the day, and with not a single person allowed inside since I arrived, a guard opens the door to let in some people. Jared and Kate squeeze in, but not me. Ten minutes later, on a second wave, I make it in, but a guard inside kicks a bunch of us back out. All looks lost.

Then Jared appears at the door, holding aloft not one passport, but two. "I've got your passport, mate," he says. "I've checked, and it's got your visa in it."

He's a gift from the Gods, delivered by bicycle. I thank him for his help, then push on to the bus station. It's on the other side of the city, and I have to negotiate a rainy rush hour for a bus departing in ninety minutes.

I get there just in time, soaked and shivering - which on a scale of one to ten for states in which to turn up for a twenty-four-hour bus ride ranks as a two, with only soaked, shivering, and stark naked being worse.

KAZAKHSTAN

URUMQI TO ALMATY

I lie in my bed on the bus, face pressed against the window, peering at a Narnia-like landscape covered in thick snow and fir trees. I look for fairies and fauns but see only sheep and horses. There's the occasional wigwam-type structure, smoke billowing from its top. Outside them stand fur-clad men, readying themselves for a day of hunting unicorns.

The scenery since leaving Sydney has varied wildly. As snapshots, the landscapes contrast as much as black and white, but they blend and merge so slowly and subtly that the transition from desert to jungle to Narnia unfolds unnoticed. Flying from place to place might be quicker, but it means missing everything in between, and there can be as much to enjoy between destinations as there is in them; like the scenery today, which is as spectacular as I've ever seen. These scenes feel a just reward for seeing through those difficult days in Urumqi, which had me questioning if this trip was worth it. This morning, seeing scenes like these, has reaffirmed it is.

The bus is driven by three chunky, stubbled Uzbekistanis, who rotate between driving and sleeping. Whoever's driving always has a cigarette on the go. The other passengers are a motley crew of Kazakhs, Uzbekistanis, and Kyrgyzstanis. One looked a proper stunner at the outset but now looks the opposite. A twenty-four-hour bus ride should be part of Miss World contests. Even I can fake it on stage in a bikini for five minutes.

On entering Kazakhstan, for hours we traverse flat, bare land; the nothingness alleviated only by the distant, cloud-covered mountains, and the odd camel. A whopper of a country, it has more space than it knows what to do with. It's the size of these countries combined: Italy, Spain, France, Norway, Sweden, Germany, and the UK.

At the bus station in Almaty, dozens of guys harass me with offers of taxis and hotels. I make a deal with one to take me to a hostel. When I'm in the taxi, I realise it's not a taxi, just a man who owns a car. Fearing that he might be planning to rob me, I jut out my chin and growl - a tactic to trick people into thinking I'm a double-hard bastard. I've never been mugged, so the tactic is scientifically proven. Or muggers may just think it pointless to rob someone who seemingly can't afford shoes and a razor. He takes me to Hostel 74/76. If they couldn't choose between calling it Hostel 74 or Hostel 76, they should have split the difference and called it Hostel 75. The room costs £7 a night. I'm sharing it with two Russians and a Kazakh.

The Kazakh, Saken, invites me to go with him to Ile

Alatau, a mountain on the edge of the city. I'm not equipped for mountains, but the sun's out, and it's thirtyish degrees. A series of cable cars take us up. At 2,000 metres is Shymbulak, Central Asia's premier skiing resort. A sign displays equipment rental prices. You can hire everything you need for £15 a day. In the Alps, an apple costs £15. Heading further up, Saken tells me about a business deal he's working on: "We want to buy 2,400 cows, at £3,000 each. That's the price for a Canadian cow, which have the best genetics. At first, we'll sell the milk abroad to be processed; later we'll build a processing plant here. As well as selling the milk, we'll also breed the cows and sell some of the calves, and slaughter the old cows and sell the meat."

It sounds a good idea. When I get back to London, I'll go to the bank and ask for £6,000 to buy a couple of Canadian cows. This time next year, I'll be a millionaire - in pounds, not just kip.

The final cable car stop is Talgar Pass, at 3,200 metres. The highest peak, a hundred metres away, pokes through the clouds. The ground is thick with snow, and it's damn cold. But not arctic cold, so we go for a walk. After twenty minutes - five spent making a snow angel - my face is red, my lips have cracked, and my feet feel like stone. We take refuge on an out-of-service chairlift to get my feet out the snow. Saken asks why I haven't got a pair of trainers. "If I buy trainers, I'll have to buy socks too," I tell him. "And then a shoe rack and a sock drawer. It's a slippery slope."

On the bus back to the hostel, a guy wearing a baseball cap and baggy jeans comes over. After asking where I'm from and what I'm doing in Almaty, he says he wants to go to Los Angeles to be a rapper.

"You'll rap in English?"

"No. Rap Kazakh language."

"Why Los Angeles?"

"American girl. Big ass. Big ears."

"Big ears?"

"Yes."

"You mean big eyes?"

I point to his eyes and say "eyes", then I point to his ears and say "ears".

He pulls his ears outwards with his hands and says, "No, big ears."

Fair enough, mate; whatever floats your boat.

Later, I go to the train station to buy a ticket to Astana, the capital of Kazakhstan. The ticket seller doesn't speak English, but she puts me on the phone with a woman who speaks a little, who relays what I want back to the ticket seller. The ticket is for a day earlier than I wanted, and I don't know if I've got a seat or a bed on the train, and I think I was overcharged, but at least I've got one.

Back at the room, Saken picks up the ticket, which I left on the table. "I thought you were travelling to London without flying," he says.

"Yeah, that's what I'm doing."

"But this is a plane ticket to Astana."

I study his face to see if he's winding me up. It doesn't look like he is.

"What?! Are you sure?"

"The arrival time is an hour after the departure time. And see here, it says 'airport' in English."

"Ah, bollocks; so it does."

I didn't check the ticket after the seller gave it to me because I assumed it was all in Kazakh. I also assumed, it being a train station, that they wouldn't be selling fucking plane tickets.

ALMATY

The woman at the train station, who Saken phoned to explain the mix-up, laughs at me when I walk in. She gives me a refund and points to a row of counters five metres away. I realise the mistake I made: this is a travel agency within the train station. I'm sure dozens of people each day make the same mistake. Or maybe not; maybe I'm just an idiot. At one of the counters, I hand over a piece of paper on which Saken has written in Kazakh what I want and pay £20 for the train ticket to Astana, a twenty-hour ride away. I'll wait until I'm in Astana until I celebrate, though, in case this is a camel ticket, not a train one.

Next, I go to a metro station to head to the immigration office that foreigners have to report to within five days of entering the country. As I approach the ticket barrier, I get pulled over by a burly man in a blue uniform. I don't understand what he says other than the word "passport". I hand it to him, and he turns to the photo page. Looking confused, he gestures me to follow him. We walk down a corridor and into a small room, which has mugshots on the walls. He radios someone else to come. When his pal arrives, he shows him my passport, which he scrutinises. A discussion between the two follows, during which both look me up and down, frowning.

"UK?" the first man asks me.

"Yes."

He screws up his face in disgust as he points at my beard and flip-flops.

"London?" he asks.

"Yes."

He gives me a pitiful look and waves me away.

I blame Beckham. He's inflated the expected sartorial standards of British men abroad. Borat has perhaps had the reverse effect for Kazakh men, who when overseas get quizzed why they're not wearing a mankini.

In the queue at the immigration office, I chat to a wiry, pony-tailed Frenchman called Cedric. Imagine my surprise when he tells me he walked here from France. "I set off two years ago," he says. "I walk 25 km most days, but it can be up to 40 km if I'm low on supplies. Sometimes I camp outdoors; sometimes locals invite me to stay at their house. I've got no destination in mind. I'll just keep heading eastwards."

It sounds unbelievable, but I believe him. If you saw him, you'd also believe him. He looks like someone who's spent two years walking. He smells like it too. But I do some sums to double-check. Paris to Almaty is about 7,000 km, and he said he set off two years ago. It works out to an average of 10 km a day. It's definitely doable.

In the afternoon, I go to a spa complex called Arasan Baths. There are separate men's and women's sections, and everyone is naked - balls out, say hello to Mr Wonka naked.

I take a seat in a sauna, in which are three other guys. After a minute, two of them stand: one bends over, and the other beats the bent man's back and arse with a bundle of birch twigs. After that pair of pervs have gone, I'm left with one guy, a Carlo Ancelotti lookalike. He points at the coals and asks me something. I tell him that I'm from England, that I can't speak Kazakh.

"You think England important country? Everybody have to speak English?" he barks at me. "Your English no good here. You speak Kazakh."

We eyeball each other in silence. I think to myself, if he tries pushing my face in the coals, I'll blind him with birch twigs.

Then, like a switch has been flicked, his tone changes and I'm his new best friend. He tells me he was an officer in the Soviet Union for twenty-five years and worked in Afghanistan, Tajikistan, Germany, and Hungary. He invites me to drink tea with him. We walk out the sauna and into a cafe, each grabbing a towel on the way to wrap around our waists. He orders two beers, no tea. He downs half his beer in one go. I do the same.

"Communist life like prison life," he says. "No freedom and food not enough. But vodka, have a lot. We think it last forever, then one day, 1991, it no more. They say money finished, Soviet Union finished. I come back Kazakhstan and become businessman."

He necks the rest of his beer and orders two more.

"British people are best," he tells me. "Men are like stone. Nation of fighters, pioneers, adventurers. Look at you, here in Kazakhstan alone. Don't know language, don't know anyone, but don't care. You are good example of British."

He chugs another half glass of beer. So do I.

"Russia like angry bear," he says. "World has to beware them. They worry China, but Russia is most dangerous. I like America more. They welcome everybody. Live together in peace."

Ten minutes after sitting, having each drunk two beers, we leave the cafe and spend an hour rotating through steam rooms, saunas, and pools.

After a couple more five-minute beers and getting changed back into clothes, he says I must join him for dinner. As we eat and drink - four more beers - he talks about his shrapnel wounds, his son's wheeling and dealing in oil, and Jamie Oliver, who he thinks is the best chef in the world. He insists on paying the bill himself, and that I go to his home to meet his wife.

We drive to an estate of dreary apartment blocks on the outskirts of the city. He majorly scrapes another car while trying to park. "That was shit car, anyway," he says, with a dismissive flick of the hand towards the now even shitter car. Inside, I meet his wife and daughter, a pair of plump women. We sit at the kitchen table for a couple of hours, eating, drinking, and chatting. He's sozzled but won't hear of me getting a taxi, and drives me back to the hostel himself.

He turned out to be alright. I'm glad I didn't blind him with birch twigs.

ASTANA

My hostel is on the twelfth floor of an apartment block. I'm sharing a four-bed room with three twenty-something Kazakh guys, who rolled in at 5 am. Two of them are snoring, and the other is sleeping naked, without a sheet covering him. Among the other guests are a pair of Russian identical twins. I didn't initially realise they were twins, as I hadn't seen both of them in the same room at the same time. I thought it was one person who kept changing his clothes. There's also a Ghanian guy, who's in Kazakhstan setting up a program to cross-promote Ghana and Kazakhstan. "If we educate people about the other country," he tells me, "it will generate interest to travel there. I'll hire some rooms and show movies; this will help them learn." I'm not convinced that showing *The Lion King* in Kazakhstan and *Borat* in Ghana will help much. That said, I've watched *Borat*, and now I'm in Kazakhstan, while I've never watched *The Lion King*, and haven't visited Africa. So there might be something in it.

The Ishim River splits Astana in two, and the two sides could hardly be more different. The right side is an unremarkable, Soviet-style affair, whereas the left side is science fiction-like, with a dash of Las Vegas and a hint of Singapore. The Palace of Peace and Reconciliation is a colossal, metallic pyramid. The Bayterek Tower is a near-hundred-metre white tower topped by a golden globe. The Khan Shatyr is a tent-type structure that looks like something the Teletubbies would live in. There's also a presidential palace that looks like the White House, a flying saucer-shaped circus, a couple of egg-shaped buildings, and more skyscrapers than I can count.

Adding to the wow factor is Astana's location: in the middle of the world's largest steppe. For 1,000 km in every direction is an empty expanse. There's a clear-cut boundary where buildings and roads abruptly stop, then nothing but nothingness for as far as the eye can see.

The impressiveness of the capital is a consequence of Kazakhstan becoming a major player in oil and gas. In 2000, the world's largest oil find of the last thirty years was made in Kazakhstan's share of the Caspian Sea. It's been a warp speed change since then. Before that, Astana barely existed. Then called Akmola, it was inhabited mainly by impoverished agricultural workers, and was best known for being a former Gulag prison camp. President Nazarbayev instigated the change. Deciding the former capital, Almaty, was too close to China, he granted capital status to Akmola and forced tens of thousands of government employees to move here. A year later it was renamed Astana, which sounds like a cool name, but in Kazakh means "capital city", which is as boring as you can get.

At the Russian embassy, I'm told that to get a visa for Russia I must show proof of residence in Kazakhstan for the last ninety days. I'm seventy-nine days short of that, with nineteen days left on my Kazakh visa, so travelling to London via Russia, the most direct route, is ruled out. Kazakhstan to Azerbaijan to Georgia to Turkey to Southeast Europe is the next best option. This route hinges on getting a visa for Azerbaijan, and to get one of those I need a letter of invitation from someone in Azerbaijan. Ten minutes of

Googling tells me it's possible to buy a letter of invitation for £35. The websites selling them all seem likely to steal my identity after I send them copies of my documents, but I've no choice but to gamble on one. If they do steal my identity, I'll just steal someone else's. I quite fancy being a Jamaican woman.

I received a PDF copy of my letter of invitation to Azerbaijan, and spent yesterday locating the Azerbaijan embassy; to be told once there that the lazy sods are only open on Mondays, Wednesdays, and Fridays, and only from 3-5 pm on those days.

I'm back there again today. Instead of a bleak building swarmed by hundreds, it's a pink house with a handful of people politely queuing. In the waiting room, an old man asks, "Liverpool. Champion?"

"No. Manchester City."

A sad look crosses his face.

"Margaret Thatcher?" he asks.

When I swipe my finger over my neck to indicate she's dead, an even sadder look crosses his face. His radio must have broken in 1990, and he's yet to buy a new one.

There's no messing around with counter clerks: I'm called through to meet the head honcho, the Azerbaijan Ambassador. He's dressed like a waiter in a third-rate restaurant, and someone appears to have detonated a paper cluster bomb in his office. He checks my paperwork while fielding phone calls and signing documents brought into him. Satisfied, he tells me, "Come back after Wednesday."

"After Wednesday? So, Friday?"

"Between Wednesday and Friday."

"Thursday? But you're not open on Thursdays."

"Between Wednesday and Thursday."

A week has passed since I submitted my visa application to the Azerbaijan Ambassador. If I don't get the visa today then my chances of exiting Kazakhstan without flying drop from unlikely to no way. It's not possible to extend a Kazakh tourist visa, and there are only seven days left on mine. In that time, I need to travel the width of the country to the port city of Aktau and board a boat bound for Azerbaijan, which doesn't have a land border with Kazakhstan. I anticipate that boat being an issue. The best news I can find online is that a boat from Aktau to Azerbaijan leaves every three to fourteen days. The worst is that boats allowing passengers aboard have stopped traversing the route. Less than three weeks after dancing with defeat in Urumqi, I'm back on the ropes, facing a knockout.

At the embassy, I'm called through to see the ambassador. He waves me through the open door while he's on the phone.

"Am I getting the visa? Is it ready?" I ask after he's done on the phone.

He says nothing but delves into one of the mounds of documents on the floor. He finds my passport and flicks through it. "Your visa, hmm, I don't know," he says, with a puzzled look on his face. He delves into another mound and produces a printed slip of paper with my photo on it. He picks up a glue stick and two become one. It's game on.

Saken, the guy I made snow angels with in Almaty, lives in Astana, so I ask him to come with me to buy a ticket for the train to Aktau. With limited time, I can't afford any plane ticket mistakes. The options are a £110 first-class ticket to Atyrau in the north-west tomorrow, then another train south from there to Aktau; or wait three days for a cheaper ticket for a train direct to Aktau. It's more expensive and more hassle, but those two days saved by going via Atyrau could be crucial. I'd be gutted to reach Aktau and find I've missed the boat by a day or two, and it was penny-pinching and laziness that cost me the chance to get it. So I book the ticket to Atyrau.

ATYRAU TO AKTAU

I arrived in Atyrau yesterday afternoon, after a twenty-two-hour journey. My first-class cabin, in which I was alone, was immense. It had an en-suite toilet and shower. I felt more refreshed when I got off the train than when I got on, which is a first.

I'm back with the common people for today's train, an ex-Soviet special with dark woods, brown carpets, and ruby-red upholstery. I'm in "kupe" class which means a cabin with four beds - two below, two above. Between walks of the train - browsing cabins through open doors, glimpsing people eating, chatting, and sleeping - I spend hours looking out the window, at mainly nothing. The emptiness is interrupted only by the occasional one-horse town, all of which we stop at. At one of these, the town's one horse is temporarily joined by two-hundred-plus more, herded past by a couple of men riding bareback, brandishing heavy sticks. Any horse tempted to gallop to freedom is thwacked. They should make a run for it because they're destined for a dinner plate. Horse is the favoured meat in Kazakhstan. You won't find Kazakhs complaining if a supermarket slyly slips some horse meat into their sausages.

During one walk of the train, I meet a guy called Azamat, who invites me to his cabin to eat dumplings and drink tea. "I'm getting married in August," he tells me, "so I need to work a lot now to pay for it. Kazakh weddings are expensive because you have to invite everyone you know, even if you don't know them well. We have five hundred people on our guest list at the moment, but we expect it to be more."

He's going to a town an hour from Aktau to visit his sister, whose husband died last week in an explosion at the oil refinery he worked at. The company are refusing to pay compensation because investigators claim it was the employees' fault for being drunk at work. "He was Muslim and never once drank alcohol," says Azamat. "The company must have bribed the investigators. It's an injustice, and I won't accept it. My sister has four children. I must help them." First, he'll go to local officials to ask for assistance. If they don't help him, he'll go to the media. It's a high-risk move; one that could see him bundled into a van, never to be seen again.

Later, while having a cigarette in the end carriage of the train, a gold-toothed bloke wearing an Adidas tracksuit speaks to me. When I tell him I'm English, he taps his chest and says, "Ah, English. Me Azerbaijan. Name Roma." Shaking my hand, I notice a stitched-up wound on his. He makes a stabbing gesture to explain it, which I assume to mean someone stabbed him. I tell him I'm going to Baku in Azerbaijan, and that I'm trying to go by boat. He doesn't understand, so I draw a picture of a boat on some paper. "Me boat. Me, you, boat," he says and moves his index fingers together to indicate we can go together. "Ok, sure," I tell him, thinking he may have taken the boat before, so will improve my chances. Back in my cabin, though, paranoia kicks in. What's he involved in that would get him stabbed? Why is he taking the boat when it's faster to fly? Is he smuggling something across the border?

"Come. Taxi in," says Roma outside Aktau train station. I decide to give him a chance. What's the worst that could happen? Actually, let's not think about that. Half an hour later, the taxi stops by a small office. I recognise it from a photo in an old blog post I read when researching where to buy the boat ticket. It's no dice, though; it's boarded-up. We try a few travel agents; none sell boat tickets. Then we drive twenty minutes to the port. Roma speaks to the woman at the office there. "Boat, no. No boat. Boat no go. No go on boat," is Roma's summary of the situation.

Outside by the taxi, Roma says to me, "Give £50."

"£50? What for?"

He points at the taxi and makes the roof sign with his hands, which I guess to mean hotel. £50 seems a lot, but we've been in the taxi a long while, and I've no idea how much hotels cost here, so I hand it over. Forty-five minutes later, on the outskirts of the city, we stop outside a dump of a hostel, part-way through renovation or demolition. Roma pays the driver £15, and we go inside, where a woman takes us to a room with six beds in it. Roma hands her £10 for the two of us.

"You go shop. Buy beer," Roma says to me.

"Why don't you go to the shop and buy beer?"

"No, you," he snaps back, then adds, "please," and a wonky, golden smile.

After I get back from the shop, and we're drinking a beer in the room, he says, "Shirt I need. You give." He grabs one I've unpacked, without waiting for a reply. I don't want to argue with him, so I let it slide.

After the beer, I go to the restaurant next to the hostel. I order and sit at an outside table. Twenty minutes later, Roma shows up and sits at my table. After he's eaten, he taps his pocket and says, "Money, no. Need more."

"Where's that £50?"

"Finish. Pay taxi. Pay hotel. Give more."

"No."

"Fuck you. Give more."

His mask has more than slipped; it's gone. What's left isn't pretty. I'm not confident about taking him down in a fight, so I tell him I'll go to the room to get some and will be back in a minute.

In the room, I consider the situation: there's a bloke out there wearing one of my shirts, with a wedge of my cash in his pocket, who wants me to pay for his dinner. If it carries on like this, in a day or two - if I'm not in a ditch - I'll be down to only my pants and passport. I need to man up, grow some balls. Or pack my bag and do a runner. I do the latter: out the back door and down a dusty road.

A half hour walk brings me to the main drag. While looking for an internet cafe, I see an Irish pub called The Shamrock that has a wifi sign outside. I opt for that instead. Over a few pints, my waning morale drops further. I plumb the depths of Google but can't find any up-to-date information about the boat to Baku. After five pints, I've written it off and am on a mission to drown my sorrows.

Ordering my eighth pint at the bar, I get talking to Raymond, a fifty-something Scottish guy, who turns out to be the owner of the pub. On hearing he's lived in Aktau for eight years, I ask him if he knows anything about boats going to Azerbaijan. "There used to be a boat running between here and Baku," he says, "but I haven't heard anyone mention it in a long time. I'll make a couple of calls to see what I can find out."

The calls yield no leads.

My sorrows are drowned after ten pints, and it's time to leave. Raymond recommends I stay at the Green Hotel, and gets one of his staff to drive me there. At £35 a night, it's not cheap, but sod it. Budgeting doesn't matter anymore. My visa expires in three days. Then I'm flying home.

AKTAU

At 10 am, the ringing of the in-room phone wakes me. I don't understand what the woman on the phone says, so I go down to reception, from where she takes me to the dining room. I feel too sick to stomach breakfast, but it's easier to go with the flow. A minute after I take a seat, a broad-chested, stubble-faced man sits at my table and grins at me. He speaks, in Kazakh, into his phone and then hands it to me. Displayed is an English translation of what he said: "I manager hotel. Name Zaurbek. Is your name? Business person? City Aktau good?"

When I start to answer he indicates I should speak into the phone so that it can translate. With my crippling hangover, I'm not in the mood for this, but I can't tell the manager to go away. The Google Translate conversation goes on for twenty minutes. When I explain the journey I've been on, he says, "Think you fellows mental. Kazakhstan, no one travel much."

I'm about to excuse myself, so I can return to hiding under my duvet, when he says, "Mike, you need help ticket Azerbaijan?"

I tell him I've tried, that's there's no boat. At least not one leaving within the next few days, before my visa expires.

"Come reception thirty minutes past one hour," he says.

Forty-five minutes later, we're cruising in a black Mercedes. He's wearing shades and smoking - and still smiling. He looks like a mafioso on ecstasy. We stop outside the closed office I came to with Roma. He knocks the door and peers through the boarded-up window. After checking with a nearby office, he says, "No ticket here. Office closed before."

Ten minutes later, we're on another estate, walking in circles. My face must show defeat because he says, "Mike, worry not. You go Azerbaijan." He's called me Mike all morning. I left it too late to correct him.

We find the place he was looking for and take a seat at the desk inside. Zaurbek talks with the woman working there. She starts filling in a form.

"Ticket £65," Zaurbek tells me. "Give must passport."

"It's a boat ticket?" I ask.

"Yes, boat. Maybe today. Maybe tomorrow. Maybe three or four day."

She gives me a ticket, and we leave. It should be a joyful moment, but I'm holding back. There are only two days left on my Kazakh visa, so even though I've got a ticket, I won't be able to use it if the boat doesn't depart in the next two days.

In the evening, Zaurbek knocks my door clutching a bottle of whisky. I'm still hungover but can't refuse after the help he's given me. We engage in a drinking session downstairs. Over a few hours, we finish the bottle.

Google Translate has spewed some nonsense today, including stuff about socks, chalk, and lemons. It hits the spot now, though. As the session concludes, it translates what he says to: "As life happens, we have to help each other."

At 8 pm the next day, there's a knock on my door. Zaurbek hands me his phone: "Boat registration. Leaving soon. Come now." He drives me to the port and speaks to someone to double-check everything is okay with my ticket.

Without his help, I'd never have made it. What a legend he is.

After he leaves, I take a seat on a plastic chair in the white linoed waiting room and watch Columbia vs Ivory Coast on a battered television. Six others are here: a family of four Azeris and a couple of Kazakh guys. I keep an eye on the door, hoping Roma doesn't show up.

That was a gamble when I did a runner. I twisted and got twenty-one. Luck has been on my side: to find The Shamrock, for Raymond to send me to the Green Hotel, and for the boat to be leaving today and not in a few days time.

At 11 pm, I board the Professor Gul, a rusty ferry flying the Azeri flag. The boat is still docked as I drift to sleep. When I wake, I'll be crossing the Caspian Sea.

AZERBAIJAN

BAKU

I spent yesterday, sleepily and uneventfully, crossing the Caspian Sea. It's actually a lake - the world's largest - but the Romans called it a sea and no one has yet gotten around to renaming it. Another factoid for you: Azerbaijan is one of only two countries with a name that begins with "A" but doesn't end with "a". I'm not telling you the other. It's your homework.

My homework is to find somewhere to sleep because I arrive in Baku, the Azeri capital, without a room booked. After a drive in a Lada, a visit to an internet cafe, and two hours of walking, I find myself at a place that I'm certain is, by some distance, both the cheapest and crappiest in a city of flashy hotels and designer boutiques. The signage is "Caspian Hostel" written in black pen on a piece of wood. Access is via a creaky spiral staircase in a courtyard filled with junk. Inside is a room with seven bunks, and an adjoined kitchenette and bathroom. My roommates are a ragtag bunch from around the world: Kazakhstan, Tajikistan, Georgia, Russia, Poland, France, Japan, and Iran. There are a couple of other long-distance, non-flying travellers: one is motorcycling from Paris to Vladivostok, another is cycling from London to Melbourne. What a light-weight I am, taking trains and buses. They and I are making do with this dump because the foreigners Azerbaijan typically attracts are well-heeled ones in town on oil-related business because Azerbaijan, like Kazakhstan, has hit the black gold mother lode.

Having signed four billion pounds worth of oil contracts, and having untapped reserves estimated to be worth tril-lions more, Azerbaijan is undergoing accelerated moderni-sation to make up for the Soviets' meddling. Though keen to splash the cash, Baku's planners have been more reserved than their Astana counterparts. They've restricted them-selves to a single wacky building. The Flame Towers, on a ridge overlooking the city, are three near-two-hundred-metre buildings, each shaped to resemble a flame, to create the effect of fire.

Baku also has what was, at 162 metres, the world's tallest flagpole. It held the record for a year, until Tajikistan, the cheeky bastards, built one three metres higher. The same person designed both flagpoles. What a job that is, designing flagpoles.

I'll crack a world record myself one day. Being a lazy sod, I'd like to get it done within a minute. Realistic options include most sticky notes on a face in a minute (58), fastest time to assemble Mr Potato Head while blindfolded (16.17 seconds), and fastest time to duct tape a person to a wall (41.66 seconds).

It's the older parts of Baku that are best, not the newer ones. The highlight is Icheri Sheher, the medieval district: a labyrinth of cobbled streets and alleys, filled with teahouses, courtyards, and carpet sellers. Thousands call Icheri Sheher home, including the two kids I come upon down one of the lanes. One is wrapping the other in VHS tape, mummy-style. They see me giving them a weird look and give me one back; like I'm the odd one for not being wrapped in VHS tape. I can't really call them weird. People in glass houses and all that. Spending an afternoon wrapped in VHS tape is no stranger than spending one in a room of naked men hitting each other with birch twigs.

Walking the promenade around the Bay of Baku, I see a one-armed man and do an unintentional double-take. I pretend I wasn't looking at him, but gazing into the distance, but he knows my game. What he lacks in arms, he makes up for in smarts. I flee when he starts approaching, fearing a confrontation won't be favourable for me. I'll have to beat a disabled man or get beaten by one. Neither are outcomes I can post on Facebook. That's twice in a week I've run away from Azeris. I'll have to punch a couple before I leave the country to keep intact my reputation of being a double-hard bastard.

Groups of guys, slick-looking and dark-shaded, are plentiful along the promenade, strolling, smoking, and joking.

None of them wear shorts despite the sun being out. Perhaps they think shorts aren't cool. Possibly they've got knobbly knees. Or maybe they're Muslims - 95% of Azeris are - adhering to the Quran forbidding women and men to show their thighs. Punishable by stoning, probably. Everything else seems to be. Were I to wear shorts now, I'd deserved to be stoned. My tanned feet next to my white legs - with a distinct line where my jeans reach down to - would make it look like I'm wearing brown socks with flip-flops. A fashion crime so serious that I would throw stones at myself.

The guys eye every pretty woman who passes. None of them make a move; they just whisper and giggle to each other, like schoolboys browsing a biology textbook. I wonder how men in Muslim countries flirt with women. They can't use the standard Western approach of getting drunk, moonwalking over, and blurting, "Alright darling, can I touch your boob?" They must have to use charm. If that's the case, I'm lucky I'm not Muslim. I've got a full set of arms but was short-changed on charm. That's why I practice moonwalking every day.

Back at the hostel, I talk with a mutton-chopped, moustached Iranian, whose name I can't work out even though he's told me three times. It's maybe Farsheed, or it could be Hagid, or possibly Vagi. It should be a hostel rule for people with quirky names to wear name badges. He's buzzing about how little the local women are wearing: "One was wearing something like a nightdress. Another, who I followed for a minute, you could see her panty line. They'd get arrested in Iran for what they wear here."

I ask him what it's like to live in Iran. "Thoughts and

ideas are forced down your throat," he says. "At school, we were told you could see Muhammad's face in the moon. I thought there was something wrong with me because I couldn't see it. I have to live a dual life because I'm agnostic but can't openly renounce Islam. If you leave Islam, the Quran says you're worse than infidels who never believed in the first place. If people knew what I think about religion, it could get me killed."

The darkness of the conversation takes a turn when he strips down to his Y-fronts and starts singing and dancing:

> *"England swings like a pendulum do,*
> *Bobbies on bicycles, two by two,*
> *Westminster Abbey, the tower of Big Ben,*
> *The rosy red cheeks of the little children."*

That would get him killed in Iran. No doubt about it.

At 10 pm, a Kazakh and a Pole open a bottle of vodka in the kitchenette a couple of metres from my bed, which I'm laying in, trying to sleep. "Come drink," the Pole say to me. "We drink until Vodka finished."

I turn down the offer. I'm still hurting from the heavy boozing in Aktau. And a Pole, a Kazakh, and an Englishman drinking in a kitchenette sounds like the start of a joke that will end in tears.

The vodka party, which garnered half a dozen more participants and extended beyond one bottle to several, gets shut down at 2 am when the hostel owner comes in guns blazing, threatening to kick them out on the spot if they don't hand over the drinks and get in bed.

The woman in the bunk below the Pole wishes he had stayed out of bed because during the night he vomits on her. He denies it was him but the evidence is conclusive: a trail of sick runs down the wall from his bed to hers, sick stains cover his shirt, and sick coats his mouth. No need to call in Sherlock for this case.

GEORGIA

SIGHNAGHI

I'm at the Azerbaijan-Georgia border with Vahid, the Iranian from the hostel in Baku. Iranians - like Brits and half the world's nationalities - used to be able to get a visa-on-arrival for Georgia at the border, but that changed at some point in the last year, and no one has told Vahid until now, and the person telling him is an arsey Azeri immigration officer.

After berating Vahid for coming to the border without a visa, he asks, "You two together?"

I shuffle to the side. It's every man for himself. "Well, yes and no. Not exactly. More no," I say.

He looks through our passports again and then at Vahid. "This is you? It look not like you."

I shuffle a little bit more.

It's true that Vahid doesn't look like his passport photo.

He did until last night, when he shaved off all his facial hair, thinking it best not to resemble a terrorist when entering Georgia, a Christian country. He now looks like a twenty-something, clean-shaven lad, whereas the photo in his passport looks like a thirty-something, bushy-faced terrorist.

"I see you two come same time," says the officer. "Sit there. Wait."

We take a seat on a bench in a cordoned off area. I'm annoyed at my naivety for ignoring guideline no.476 of the official traveller handbook: "Don't enter a Christian country accompanied by an Iranian."

Thirty minutes later, the officer hands back our passports. "You no go Georgia. Leave now," he says.

"I'm from the UK. I don't need a visa for Georgia. You have to let me through," I say on repeat, refusing to leave.

Making a fuss isn't advisable when dealing with officials from countries with names that end in "an", but the situation calls for it. The alternatives to Georgia are Iran and Russia, for which I'll need visas that are difficult or impossible to get.

A more senior-looking official, who's been watching the scene through an office window, comes to see what's going on. He takes my passport, tells me to sit again, then disappears somewhere. When he returns, he hands my passport to the arsey officer and says something to him. The officer, moodily and reluctantly, points through the barrier to Georgia.

Vahid lifts his head from his hands and looks at me. He has no chance of getting through - short of telling them he's wearing a suicide vest, which would cause other problems later on. There are no words of consolation worth saying, so I just give him a nod. He nods back, and I leave.

En route to Sighnaghi, I pass grand castles, quaint churches, and ancient watchtowers, scattered around mountain-backed pastures and vineyards in every shade of green. It's like Bilbo's Shire, but with fewer hobbits. Outside crumbling houses with overgrown gardens, rusty tractors stand idle; tired Ladas too. Their owners sit on stools beside buckets of melons, tomatoes, and peaches. Particularly peaches. There are shitloads of peaches.

The remnants of eighteenth-century fortifications surround Sighnaghi, a picturesque settlement perched on a thickly foliaged slope of the Tsiv-Gombori mountain range, overlooking the Alazani Valley. In the town square, locals sell fresh produce: bowls of onions, buckets of pears, plates of cucumbers, handfuls of tomatoes, and stacks upon stacks of peaches. Other locals loiter around a fountain swigging wine.

I'll also be making an early start on the booze, with a wine tasting and sightseeing tour. People don't associate Georgia with wine, but the word itself comes from the Georgian word "g'vino", and the world's oldest wine making equipment was found here. So Georgia is the home of wine, not Italy or France. That's what the Georgian Tourism Board are peddling anyway.

There are only four of us on the tour, including the tour guide, Goga. The other two are an Israeli couple on their honeymoon. Just what they want on their romantic wine tasting tour: me. The first two stops are monasteries; only a couple of the numerous religious buildings in the region. While most European countries have seen religious fervour decline in recent decades - with younger generations favouring sex, drugs, and rock 'n' roll - Christianity in Georgia is as popular as ever. Three-quarters of Georgians regularly attend church.

Back on the road, we pass mounds of mouldy, manky peaches outside every other house in every other village. "In Georgia, we have nice peaches," Goga explains, "but now we have too many. Before, Russian people like buy Georgian peaches. Now Georgia and Russia do no business. Russian people can't enjoy our nice peaches. Georgian people can't make money from sell our nice peaches. It shame for everyone."

The next stop is the Khareba Winery, home to the country's largest wine cellar. The cellar is carved into the Caucasus Mountains in the form of 8 km of tunnels, built by the Soviets during the Cold War for military purposes. 25,000 bottles of wine are stored in the dark, dank tunnels. If the Cold War heats up again, I'm coming here to sit it out. If five mates and I came and limited ourselves to two bottles each a day, those 25,000 would last us five years, by which point the radioactivity will have cooled, and the pubs will have re-opened.

Returning to Sighnaghi, Goga pulls over in one of the villages and gets out of the car to argue with one of its locals. Back in the car, he says, "This man owe money to my friend for long time. I tell him this no good. He must pay money back my friend. He say he have no money to give. He say my friend can have some car wheel. He say car wheel he have, but money he no have. I call my friend, but he say he no want car wheel."

I'm staying in a dorm room at the Nato & Lado Guesthouse for £5 a night. It's run by a guy, Lado, and his daughter, Nato, who have turned the family home into a guesthouse. Nato invites me to join her and her family for dinner. They're sat at a table outside, eating and drinking - mainly drinking. "Sit, eat, drink," she says. "In Georgia, we say every guest is sent by God."

Everyone's glass is filled with wine poured from clay jugs. "This is Georgian white wine. It's the original and best wine in the world," says Nato, before making a toast to friendship between England and Georgia. Glasses are clinked to cries of "gaumarjos!" - Georgian for "cheers" - and everyone downs their drink. I'm handed a plate with juicy lumps of lamb, another with salted tomatoes and cucumbers, and another with thick, crusty bread. Before I can tuck in, the glasses are refilled with wine. "Gaumarjos!" The glasses are emptied.

Lado stands and says, "Cha cha?" Everyone cheers, and he goes into the kitchen. Rather than returning in Spandex and dancing shoes, he comes back with a tray of tumblers containing chacha, a 50+% proof spirit made from grape residue. "Gaumarjos!" And it's down in one. It tastes similar to Italian grappa - so say the Georgian Tourism Board. But paint stripper is a more accurate description.

Next, khinkali is served, traditional Georgian dumplings

filled with meat. The way to eat them is to hold the pinched part at the top, bite a bit off the bottom, suck the juice out, and then eat the rest. It's not as easy as it sounds, especially after wine and chacha. I'm messier than a spastic with a jammy doughnut.

Then it's wine refills all round and a toast to our ancestors. "Gaumarjos!" And another necking.

Twenty minutes later, after a toast to Georgia joining Europe, and the requisite "gaumarjos!", I try to get away with sipping my wine instead of finishing it in one, but I get called out on it. "In Georgia, men must drink the full glass when toasting. If not drink all, not real man," Lado tells me.

I am a real man, and I'll bloody show him so. "Gaumarjos!" And it's gone.

After several more "gaumarjos!" I'm hoping the wine is nearly finished; however: "This wine is from our vineyard," says Nato. "We have barrels of it here. It's on tap in the kitchen."

By 10 pm, having set a new personal best for wine consumption, I feel myself teetering on total wipeout, so I go to bed. I lay there, half-dead, mumbling to myself: "Gaumarjos! Gaumarjos! Gaumarjos!"

TBILISI

Tbilisi, the capital of Georgia, a hundred kilometres from Sighnaghi, hasn't had oil money to get itself a post-Soviet outfit, so I was expecting it to be grey and grim but it's not. It's part ghetto, part heritage site, with a dousing of bohemian.

A mishmash of uniformly dilapidated buildings lean and skew along tree-shaded streets. Few have seen renovation or redecoration in decades. Paint peels off plaster that's crumbling off cracked brickwork. That's if they're built from brick; some are made from wood. Some have unhinged doors opening onto mangled, twisted stairwells - the type people go up in horror movies but never come back down. Others have tunnel-like driveways through their frontage, accessed through broken, wrought iron gates, leading into communal courtyards. Some look like write-offs, with a wall on the verge of collapse, or the upper floor missing. Yet even in the worst of the worst, signs of life show in the windows: a twitch of a curtain, a ghost of a shadow. There's colour in the form of facades painted in faded pastels, and striking graffiti sprayed on every surface. People can't be bothered to clean it off, knowing they would wake to a fresh batch the following morning, which might look worse, be more offensive. Also colourful are the cut-and-shut, patched-up cars parked in the streets. Their owners haven't always gotten new parts in the same style or colour as the originals. Someone has taken the bonnet from a yellow Trabant and put it on their red Lada.

On one street, a gaggle of scruffy children hover outside a semi-stylish restaurant. They wait for a couple to stop to browse the menu, then one of them clings to the man's leg, arms and legs wrapped around vice-like. The man tries but fails to shake off the kid. Then a couple of the other kids start being noisy and dancing around the man; to draw more attention to the scene. Red-faced, the man gives them money to detach from his leg and leave him alone. They do so, then repeat the trick on another sucker minutes later. It's an effective tactic. I'll use it if I run out of cash before reaching London. An unsuspecting American tourist will be stood photographing the Berlin Wall, and then wham! I'll be clamped to his leg, demanding a £50 release fee.

In the afternoon, I visit a market spread across a bridge over the Kura River. A hundred-plus sellers display their wares on tables or blankets. Notable items include a trolley wheel, a mermaid Barbie, a doll with no arms, a pair of mismatched ballet pumps, and a vinyl album of Chubby Checker's *16 Greatest Hits*. There are countless collections of coins and badges, once prized and treasured, now flogged for pennies; and enough medals to convince people you single-handedly defeated the Nazis at Stalingrad. Lots of items bear the moustachioed face of Stalin, ruler of the Soviet Union for a quarter of a century and one of the most murderous dictators in history. The Soviet Union screwed Georgia, but don't break out the tissues because Stalin was Georgian. It makes Georgians complaining about Stalin the same as people who crap their pants and then complain about the smell. They've only got themselves to blame.

Georgia left the Soviet Union in 1991, and have since been cosy with the US and the EU. Pissed off at being dumped, Russia sought revenge in 2008 when they went to war with Georgia over South Ossetia. Georgia conceded in less than a month, losing a chunk of their territory as a consequence. Still, respect to them for taking on the might of the Russians, who they had no chance of beating. It reminds me of the time I squared up to a big guy in a pub because he tried to steal my chair; then, after him hitting me, letting him have the chair. Diplomatic relations between Georgia and Russia ended after their skirmish, with a trade embargo enforced too. Hence the millions of mouldy peaches in Georgia.

TURKEY

GOREME

I arrived in Turkey yesterday with an easy to get eVisa. It was my first overnight journey without a bed since Thailand. Despite the lack of beds, the bus was pretty damn cool. It had free wifi and screens on the back of each seat. I'd have paid a fortune for such luxuries on the thirty-five-hour bus ride I took in Australia.

Today, I'm up at 4 am to watch the sunrise and a bunch of hot-air balloons rising with it. Mikel, a roommate from the hostel, has talked me into this, which is contrary to my never-do-anything-before-nine-in-the-morning policy. He's another long-distance traveller who makes me look like a lightweight. "I've been travelling, mainly cycling, for two and a half years," he tells me. "From Goreme, I'm cycling to Tehran in Iran."

Knowing that cyclists have a penchant for skintight shorts, I warn him that Iran has a strict policy about visible panty lines. "Burn all your pants at the border," I tell him. "Better to be safe than sorry."

We go to the highest point in town and stand in the dark like a couple of lemons until, at 5.30 am, the sun emerges and seventy or so balloons ascend over the flat-topped Mount Aktepe, bouncing off each other and jockeying for position. The balloons and sunrise over the lunar-looking landscape make for a stunning spectacle.

It's the landscape, formed by volcanic eruptions, weathering, and erosion, that attracts people to Goreme. It's as close to the moon as anyone who isn't an astronaut can get. The fairy chimneys are a standout feature: hollowed-out mounds of rock resembling oversized termite nests. People used to live in them; some still do. Others lived in room-like caves carved into rock faces. A sign says they're more than a thousand years old. Some have the whole front side open; others have Flintstones-style windows and doors. Storage space is chiselled into the walls, there are stone benches to sit on and tables to eat at, and holes in the floor for cooking - possibly shitting. I'm impressed. If they had curtains and wallpaper I could see myself living in one of these - and it's one of the few apartments in the world within my price range.

In the nearby town of Kaymakli, they take the strange accommodation a step further: an eight-storey underground complex of homes, chapels, wineries, and stables connected by dozens of kilometres of tunnels. Built in the Byzantine-era as a hideout from marauding armies, locals from towns in the region took refuge in it via secret entrances. Each room has multiple passageways leading up, down, left, or right from it, creating a sense of a warren. Even with lights and directional arrows, it's confusing to navigate. Saddam Hussein should have made this his hiding place. With a multipack of fun-size Mars Bars, he could have survived for decades. I have to crouch to pass through the tunnels connecting the rooms. At one point I get bookended by a couple of fatties. If they get stuck and block me in, there won't be a moral quandary. I'll set fire to one with my lighter, and turn the fat to ash.

Back in Goreme, I see a signpost pointing down a sandy track to a place named Love Valley, so called because it contains a row of rocks shaped like penises. Half a kilometre along the track is a man selling fresh juice and tourist tat. Next to him is a path down a steep slope into the valley.

"Not good in this footwear," he says, pointing at my flip-flops. "Better you have juice and relax."

"I'll be ok. I'm a flip-flop ninja."

A few metres down, though, I'm slipping and sliding, struggling to stay upright. The man grins as he looks down at me.

"How far is this path?" I ask.

"One hour to finish. For you, more."

"And it's all like this?"

"More or less."

"Sod that."

I'll just have a juice and relax. I don't want my headstone to read: "RIP Mark Walters. Died 20th July 2014 while looking for statues of cocks."

Heading back to the hostel, a local lad stood beside a camel calls out to me: "You take photo on camel. £2 if camel sit. £3 if camel stand. £6 if camel walk." The £2 option will do. It's being on a camel that counts, not what the camel is doing. If he had a dead camel option for £1, I'd have taken that. While sat on the camel, I think to myself that it's got a better job than I have. If I were paid the same rates to sit, stand, and walk, I'd be a rich man.

In the evening, I climb a hill and stand admiring the view over the town. A man comes and stands beside me. After a few pleasantries, he invites me to his house to drink tea. Free tea is an offer an Englishman can't turn down. He lives in a luxury house, with three terraces and an interior courtyard. It's even got a proper toilet rather than a hole in the floor.

While sipping tea on one of the terraces, he tells me he's slept with women from all over the world. I eye him incredulously, thinking it a dubious claim from a man with a bulging belly; yellowed, crooked teeth; and shoulder-length, scraggly hair. "They not young or pretty women," he explains. "They fifty years or older, and fat too. Because they old and fat, they less fussy. I go the beach or pool in Bodrum and tell old, fat women they beautiful. They not beautiful, but they like hear this."

Later, the conversation takes an uneasy turn: "Why you do nothing for help Palestine?" he says. "But even you don't help, in less than fifty years Muslims come together and end Israel forever. We have defeat you invader many time before. England, France, Russia, and more have try and fail for take Turkey. You come with weapon, but we win with just hands and stones and strong hearts. Now Turkey very strong. We have much oil, but we keep secret. We don't steal oil same like America. They start war for oil. They weak. They no heart. Allah will crush them."

He continues along the same lines for fifteen minutes, his demeanour deteriorating, becoming deranged. I start to worry that he's drugged my drink. When he says, "Wait here, I go get something," and goes inside the house, I look down from the terrace to see if I can jump if I need a swift exit. It's a five-metre drop.

It turns out alright, though: he returns with a pair of binoculars to spy on women in nearby hotels.

ISTANBUL

Istanbul, a ten-hour bus ride from Goreme, is the only city in the world located on two continents - Asia and Europe. I'm staying on the European side of the city, which means I've finally left Asia after entering it five months ago on a cargo ship from Australia.

In Taksim Square, the centre of Istanbul, a colossal Turkish flag flies, skewers of kebab meat sizzle, and ranks of riot police patrol. They're mean-looking bastards: built like rugby players, dressed in black, wearing helmets. Give them capes, and they'd be a death squad of Darth Vaders. They're the rapid response regiment, in case it kicks off as it did in 2013 when a hundred thousand protesters took over Istanbul for a week. They were some of the many Turks unhappy with the Prime Minister, Erdogan, over his refusal to resign and relentless Islamification of Turkey, which is officially a secular state.

Vahid the Iranian told me - and he knows more about

such matters than most - that you can tell if a country is a dictatorship, or being run like one, if there are lots of images of the leader, of larger than poster size, when it's not election time. On that basis, Erdogan has dictator-style aspirations. His not particularly pleasant face is plastered large on walls and billboards everywhere. There are also vans with his face stuck on the side playing repetitive tunes containing his name, with guys stood next to them handing out flyers with his face on.

Off Taksim Square leads Istiklal Avenue, Istanbul's busiest street. On weekends, three million people a day pass along it; some of them on an old, red tram, taking passengers from one end to the other for £1 - or for free if you're willing, as some are, to cling on the back. Halfway along Istiklal Avenue, past the diverse jumble of boutiques and bookstores, cafes and patisseries, music stores and antique shops, is the Galata Tower: a cylindrical, cone-topped stone tower built in the fourteenth century. Better than the tower, though, is the four-level-high, bird-box-style house for cats beside it. Twenty furballs at a time can sleep in the cat condo. It's needed because Istanbul has so many cats. It should be called Istancat rather than Istanbul. I've seen a million cats but no bulls. The city's cats are well-fed and well-groomed, with locals taking joint care of them. I wish that were the case in Bournemouth, where I went to university. One day, a stray cat shat in our hallway. Everyone in the house denied it was their job to clean it up, so it was left there for a week, discolouring the carpet. I bet there are no cat shit stained hallways in Istanbul.

On the banks of the Bosporus, I sit on a bean bag under

a tree at an open-air teahouse to drink £0.50 teas from tulip-shaped glasses and eat squares of pomegranate Turkish delight sprinkled with coconut. Others mill about waiting for ferries, eating fresh fish sandwiches and drinking pickled juices. £1 for a ride to Asia? What a deal. Oh, hold on; it's only over there. Men line both sides of the Galata Bridge that crosses the river; fishing lines dangling below, fag ends discarded behind. Some have wooden contraptions attached to the bridge, holding their rods in place. No one is using a Thai-style fishing net, flinging himself off the bridge to collect his haul.

The other side of the river, Sultanahmet, is home to the Blue Mosque, Turkey's holiest building. A bulbous dome sits at its centre, above sub-domes layered below, and towering minarets line its sides. Within, twenty thousand hand-painted, ceramic, blue tiles adorn its walls. In the courtyard, men and women wash their faces, hands, and feet, cleansing themselves before entering to cleanse their souls. Lots of the women wear the niqab, only their eyes and nose visible.

Many in the West think it's wrong that Muslim women have to cover up, but it depends on what they're covering. If she has a face like a gurning bulldog, it might be the best thing for her. I've considered, for an experiment, wearing a niqab in a Muslim country to see how I get treated, with them assuming I'm a woman. If I were really committed, I could follow it all the way through to marriage. The unlucky chump wouldn't know until our wedding night that he'd married a bearded cock-and-balls-bearer.

With it being Ramadan, the streets are busier at night

than they are in the day. Locals lay low until sunset, then pull out the stops at night, once re-energised with a belly full of food. Groups in teahouses mingle and chat, sharing shishas among them. Some people are boozing, but most aren't. You don't need to drink to feel part of the festival-like atmosphere. Stalls line the street, selling fresh bagels, stuffed mussels, and roasted chestnuts. Sweet shops entice with red, green, and yellow delights stacked sumptuously in their windows. Ice cream sellers wearing waistcoats and fezzes, and brandishing half-metre spoons, exhibit more showmanship than a mixologist. Bassy beats from bars fuse with the tunes of troupes of street musicians playing horns, banjos, and saxophones. Celebratory crowds link arms and dance in circles, whooping and cheering. It's better than Christmas Eve.

I love Istanbul; its eclectic populace, bustling vibrancy, and sensuous atmosphere. If you twist my arm, I might even say it's my favourite of all the world's cities. I might quit the trip and live out my days here: sipping tea, stroking cats, and shopping for niqabs.

BULGARIA

SOFIA

I get off the bus at 5 am into the chilly pitch-black. After four hours of walking - the first three hours and fifty-five minutes of them spent looking for a hostel and a bureau de change - I sit on a broken bench in a foul park and take stock of what I've seen so far. A bag of shite is a suitable summary.

I began my morning roaming singing to myself:

> *"I'm back in the EU EU,*
> *You don't know how lucky you are boy,*
> *Back in the EU,*
> *Back in the EU,*
> *Back in the EU EU."*

Then I decided it wasn't necessary to change the words. Sofia looks more like part of the USSR than it does of the EU, which Bulgaria joined in 2007. I don't know how they got into the EU. It's in the same ballpark as Girls Aloud letting the ginger one join.

Sofia was under Turkish rule - in its Ottoman Empire guise - for five hundred years until the Soviets "liberated" the country in 1878, but any evidence of that has long gone. There's no Turkish delight. There are no cats. Blockish, monotone architecture is ubiquitous, and impressive landmarks are lacking. The National Palace of Culture, meant to celebrate the country's culture, is a colourless concrete building, chipped, cracked, and covered with graffiti. It radiates dourness, is sprinkled with depression. Grimy tiles cascade through the park in front of the "palace". I guess it used to be a water feature, but it's now waterless and weedcoated. Around it are pieces of junk art which are more junk than art. Anyone but a pretentious art wanker would class them as just junk.

If Sofia were a person, it would be a down in the gutter crackhead. Imagine such a person wearing a tie; a Primark one bought in a post-Christmas sale, that's since acquired several stains. Vitosha Boulevard, cutting through the city centre, is Sofia's tie. The paving along Vitosha Boulevard is yellow, and although this is no magical Land of Oz, there are a lot of scarecrows: scrawny specimens with haggard expressions. Decades of low wages (£275 is the monthly average) and hardcore drinking (Bulgaria ranks sixth in Bloomberg's Global Vice Index) will do that to a person. I sympathise with the locals who have migrated westwards, of which there have been many. Bulgaria is one of not many countries suffering from negative population growth: down from nine million in the late eighties to seven million today.

Thinking I've perhaps been harsh, that it has some hidden beauty, I search online for articles about Sofia. There aren't many of them. Possibly Google's SafeSearch feature has filtered most out due to writers using expletives. I have to double-check that the one saying Sofia is angling for the title of European Capital of Culture 2019 wasn't published on April 1st. The positive articles there are focus on two points: Sofia is cheap and non-touristy. It's true that it's one of the cheapest capital cities in Europe; however, it's not cheaper than Istanbul or Tbilisi. As for non-touristy, the shittiness is the reason tourists don't come. Coventry is non-touristy; it's not a reason to go there.

A few articles recommend the golden-domed Aleksandar Nevski Cathedral, so I visit there and, to be fair, it's relatively impressive. It's worthy of a photo at least, which takes my Sofia photo tally to three. The other two are of the "palace" (in case no one believes how terrible it is), and the inside of a metro station (because I've never seen so many scarecrows indoors). The cathedral, nice as it is, isn't sufficient to salvage Sofia. It's like saying Stalin once saved a kitten. One positive point can't distract from the other output.

I spend the afternoon hopping on random trams, optimistically hoping to find some cool stuff in the suburbs. But the suburbs are as skanky as the centre. There's no twist in this tale. I'm here now, though, I tell myself; I should make the most of it. But an hour later, with thoughts of suicide swirling, I do what any smart Bulgarian has already done: leave - writing off the money I paid for the hostel in the process.

SERBIA

GUCA

"It's the world's biggest trumpet festival. Or maybe it's just Serbia's biggest trumpet festival. Or it might just be a big trumpet festival." That's how it was sold to me last night. On hearing the pitch, I thought there's no way I'm going there. But many beers later I was in the frame of mind that drunk people get into when even the worst idea sounds fantastic. Which is why now, hangover hanging heavy, I'm on a bus pulling into Guca, a rural village three hours from Belgrade, being greeted by a mass of people and a barrage of trumpets.

In the centre of the village is a golden statue of a trumpeter. A man wearing a yellow helmet stands atop the statue with a snake around his neck. Below him, people clamber to take up positions for photos. Below them, a heaving crowd throw shapes and neck beers. Their states of inebriation range from smashed to paralytic. The festival is sponsored by Jelen, a brand of beer, and everyone has at least one can in hand, bought from one of the many stalls selling them for £0.70. Other stalls sell Serbian flags, military regalia, and plastic trumpets; and others food, with plumes of smoke wafting from rustic spit-roasts. This makeshift market triples the size of the village. The noise is deafening. Dozens of brass bands compete for eardrums, and hundreds of bull-horn speakers blare upbeat folksy tunes. There are no singers; not a single one.

Later there's a parade, where the bands come together for a semi-organised procession around the village. It's organised in that they follow each other in line. It's unorganised in that each band plays whatever tune they want, with scant regard for what those in front and behind are playing. The men wear winklepickers with upturned toes, grey trousers tucked into pulled-up black socks, and a coloured sash denoting where they're from. The women wear wenches outfits, with flowered aprons and ballet-like shoes. As I'm watching the parade, a man tells me, "The trumpet is important in Serbia culture. It is number one sound of country. First time, 1961, this festival very small, but this festival number fifty-four, and now famous in the world. It is honour for trumpet player come Guca. They come from everywhere: Macedonia, Slovenia, and Moldova."

Some aren't interested in the parade: pissed-up, tub-thumpers with Serbia flags wrapped around their shirtless, tattooed torsos. They ape about singing patriotic songs with great pride but little tune. With testosterone flowing as freely as the beer, scuffles break out. One is at a restaurant: a man is thrown to the floor and stamped on by three baboons. If I walked around with a "Kosovo Is Independent" slogan on my shirt, I'd get punched. I wouldn't even chance wearing an England football shirt because Serbs have reason not to be fond of foreigners: in 1999 Serbia was hit with NATO's largest strike to date. It was the first time NATO used military force against a nation that posed no threat to any of its members. They've since gone on to do that whenever the leader of a rogue country has so much as farted.

In the evening, the stars of the trumpet world battle for supremacy in a stadium. But I stick to the market because the stadium is rammed. Besides, if the Messi of trumpeters stuck his brass in my ear, I'd appreciate it no more than if a drunkard stuck a plastic trumpet in my ear and played *Agadoo*. As a finale, I try to ascend the golden statue - not an easy task when you're drunk. A Serb reaches his hand down to help pull me up. I only make it to the first base of the statue, but that will do. From my not-so-lofty position, I play the air-trumpet to the hordes below, who go wild for my tunes.

The festival itself is great; where I'm sleeping, not so much. Fifteen people and I are staying at the house of a local family, who have rented out every bed, chair, and corner of their humble abode. Another dozen are camped in their garden. For all the guests staying in the house and garden, there's a single, lockless bathroom to share. I go in there well past midnight thinking I'll finally be able to have a shower but find a man asleep on the toilet - pants around his ankles, dead to the world. I don't fancy showering with him here. If the noise startles him, the shock of seeing his pants down and me naked might lead him to the wrong conclusion, and he'll strangle me with the shower cord. So I go to bed without so much as a wash, more dishevelled than I was after even the Laos to China twenty-four-hour bus trip. I've plumbed depths unseen beyond the sphere of the homeless.

AUSTRIA

VIENNA

The Austrian capital is classy, breathing a sense of style and sophistication. Show me a person who says otherwise, and I'll show you an idiot. Astana in Kazakhstan had its fill of landmarks, but they were modern and brash, whereas Vienna's are aged and chic. Vienna is to Astana what Madonna is to Miley Cyrus. From a distance, the facades look grand; close up, they look even better, with faces, angels, horses, lions, eagles, emblems, twirls, and curls artistically entwined into their design. Nothing has been done on the cheap; there are no monotone monstrosities. The Indian and Chinese tourists lap it up. The Bulgarians too; they can't believe it. They stand wide-eyed and slack-jawed, comparing the splendour of Vienna to the shite of Sofia.

The centrepiece of the city's skyline is the 135-metre steeple of its cathedral, a building of such importance that for a long time none other in the country was legally allowed to be taller than it. They've reneged on that policy, but even now it remains the tallest building in central Vienna. Near the cathedral is the Renaissance-style Opera House, outside which powder-faced, wig-wearing touts clad in blue and gold outfits attempt to persuade passing tourists that their Mozart tour is better than the Mozart tours being offered by the hundred identically kitted-out touts stood beside them. One tout tells me Mozart performed to royalty here at the age of six. I wasn't even toilet trained at six.

The Hofburg Palace is another of Vienna's showpieces. It housed the Austrian royal family for six hundred years and is the current residence and workplace of the President of Austria. No expense has been spared on its eight wings. It makes the White House look like a prefab. Lots of Vienna's balls - there are more than four hundred per year - take place here. Locals don their finest tuxes and gowns to twirl and whirl under chandeliers to the sounds of an orchestra. If there's one tonight, I'll fashion a tux from a bin bag and dance the night away with an Austrian princess. Or any Austrian who'll have me. In the grounds of the palace, olden-days carriages pulled by horses whipped by suited and booted, bowler-hatted blokes take tourists around for the price of a pony. The horses sport cloaks and hats that match the colour of the carriage they're pulling. They're better turned out than I am, even when you factor in their rear-end nappy.

The Hofburg Palace's sister is the Schönbrunn Palace, one of the most ostentatious structures I've ever seen. The yellow-coloured 1,440-room stunner was built by the ruling family of the time to be their summer residence, 5 km from where they lived the rest of the year. That's what you call a superfluous splurge. In Europe, no one builds extravagant structures and landmarks for the sake of it anymore. With the collapse of empires, and selfish citizens demanding money be spent on them, only sensible, practical buildings get put up these days. When people a few hundred years from now are on sightseeing tours of Europe, photographing the shopping centres and office blocks that are the sum total of our architectural accomplishments, they'll think we - the people of the twentieth and twenty-first centuries - were a bunch of tight-arsed, boring bastards.

The class of Vienna, though, goes beyond fancy facades, landscaped lawns, and hat-wearing horses. There are no ticket barriers nor ticket inspectors on the trams and metro, and the public toilets are nicer than some of the rooms I've slept in. There was a piano in one of them. The bins are metallic and bullet-shaped. They look so little like bins that I walked with an empty bottle for an hour without realising that's what they were. And there's the tap water: it comes from springs in the Alps. Those are just some of the classy touches in a city full of them. It deserves its top spot in Mercer's 2014 Quality of Living Report, which ranked it above all other cities in the world.

Back at the hostel, passing time in the common room until the group of guys doing shots in my dorm go out for the night, I look online to find out how Austria - a country outside the hundred largest in the world - has managed to punch above its weight and create a stately capital of splendour. The answer is that for nearly half of the last millennium, the House of Habsburg, one of the most powerful royal houses of Europe, was based in Vienna. They pimped out princes and princesses all over Europe, who went on to become rulers of other lands, and sent money back to the motherland. Then, not long after the Habsburgs were dethroned, Vienna became the capital of the Austro-Hungarian Empire - at the time, the second largest country in Europe, and one of the world's superpowers. Vienna was pumped with money the empire plundered.

Hours later, the pissed-up partiers are still in my room. With sleep not an option, I try to get some work done. Working in Vienna conjures thoughts of luxurious lounges and slick suits. For me, however, it involves taking my laptop to the only quiet place in the hostel: a toilet cubicle.

CZECH REPUBLIC

PRAGUE

Despite once being part of the Eastern Bloc, Prague is more Vienna than Sofia. Cobbled streets lined with colourful, characterful shops, houses, and restaurants snake across the city's Old Town, past baroque, renaissance, and art nouveau structures adorned with sculptures and coats of arms. A perimeter of pastel-coloured buildings border Old Town Square, which has the gothic towers of the Tyn Church as its showpiece. In huts at its edge, slabs of pork turn over burning blocks of wood and pastries are rolled through piles of sugar. At tables outside overpriced restaurants, tourists drink coffee if they're a couple, beers if they're on a stag party.

Other tourists gather around the medieval astronomical clock. There are two faces on the clock, each with a complex combination of numbers, pictures, and hands, that tell you not only the time, but the month, the position of the moon, and what you're having for breakfast tomorrow. On the hour, coloured models built into the clock come to life, and a trumpeter appears at the top of its tower to play a jolly tune to the crowds below, who clap and cheer in excess of what his playing abilities deserve. I think going to Guca has turned me into a trumpet snob. Legend has it that the man who designed the clock had his eyes burnt out with a hot poker to prevent him building a better clock for another country. Peeved about this, the clockmaker threw himself into the innards of the astronomical clock, breaking the clock and killing himself. It took a hundred years to repair, so the clockmaker had the last laugh. Though, that laugh might have sounded more like a scream, as the clock slowly churned him into bite-sized chunks.

A short walk from the square is Charles Bridge, a four-teenth-century, sixteen-arch structure lined with statues of kings of yore, which connects Old Town with Mala Strana on the other side of the Vltava River. Crossing the bridge, you take in a scene composed of Mala Strana's baroque, red-roofed buildings; the soaring spires of St. Vitus's Cathedral; the majestic castle complex; and a hillside vineyard. "Storybook" and "fairytale" are accurate descriptions. You can make-believe you've travelled back in time, that you're a Bohemian princess in the 1300s. But then a tour group appears, resembling a whale-shaped zombie horde, looking for buildings to photograph instead of flesh to chew, and the moment is lost. You're no longer a princess, just a grown man in a Cinderella costume.

Mala Strana is much like Old Town, but has a bonus too: a castle. It sits atop a steep hill, which I have to hike with a stonking hangover. Hills and hangovers are like farts and elevators - best kept apart. The reward is a castle better than most. Covering 70,000 square metres, it's a whopper. A record breaker, actually: *Guinness World Records* ranks it as the largest castle in the world. And it's in excellent condition for something constructed a millennium ago. Outside the castle, blue-uniformed, stone-faced guards stand to attention, bayonet-tipped rifles by their side. I wonder what they're thinking, stood there for hours on end: "Are my flies undone? I wish they'd install an escalator on that hill. If one of those drunk stags on a Segway comes within a metre of me, I'll shoot the fucker in the face."

The spectrum of tourists walk around the castle: shouty Asians with selfie sticks and umbrellas, following flag-waving tour guides; bored teenagers on school trips, unsure how to fill the hour they've been given here when all there is to do is look at old stuff; and red-eyed, hungover backpackers, passing the time until it's a respectable drinking hour. "No, Simon. Don't look at that. It's not on our list. You're wasting time. We need to find number four," says one woman, a devotee of the tourism-by-numbers philosophy, and also the give-your-husband-a-hard-time-even-when-he's-on-holiday one. Another woman appears to have a door fetish. She's intent on photographing every door here.

"Mom, come on. It's just another door."

"No, this one has a flower design on it. And wow, look at that one over there too."

"Mom!"

One tourist not able to appreciate the divine doors is the man walking around with a white cane. If I were blind, I wouldn't bother going sightseeing. Once you've not seen one, you've not seen them all. I'd spend my days at home, wanking. Already being blind means it would be risk-free fun.

After being at the castle for half an hour it starts raining. European weather really sucks. I can't cope with it. I think I'm transethnic: an Asian trapped in a European's body. One day I'll move to Bangkok and have surgery to make me the Asian I've always known I am.

With sightseeing dampened, I visit an absinthe cafe. U Tri Bubnu Absintherie has shelf after shelf of the 60% proof anise, fennel, and wormwood-tasting drink on offer. It can be had neat or in a coffee, cocktail, or ice cream. I order an absinthe coffee, which is more coffee than absinthe. The sensible police can't arrest me for that. Absinthe is nick-named "The Green Fairy"; partly because it's green, partly because the hallucinogenic effects are said to make you see fairies. But it doesn't really contain psychoactive substances; that was a myth started by wine and beer makers unhappy with absinthe infringing on their market share. Still, poets, authors, and painters, like Wilde, Picasso, and Van Gogh, claim the drink inspired their best work. If it's good enough for them, it's good enough for me. I spend fifteen minutes scrawling a poem on a napkin. I'll be in profit if I can sell it for even £3, as the drink cost less than that.

> *"A flip-flopped man called Mark,*
> *Travelled by bus, train, and ark,*
> *From Sydney to London,*
> *He thought he was done,*

But then got swallowed by a shark."

Any takers? £3? No. £0.30? No. £0.03? Yes, sold to the fairy in the corner.

It's not only me drinking early and drinking a lot in Prague - everyone is at it. Czechs love beer as much as the Chinese do cigarettes. It's an integral part of the culture. While the French swirl and sniff their drinks, the Czechs take a different approach: they neck theirs and do so by the barrel. At an average of 160 litres per person, more beer is consumed per capita in the Czech Republic than anywhere else in the world. Belgium? Fannies. Germany? Lightweights. England? Shandy drinkers. It's due in part to the price. The average cost of a beer in a Czech pub is £1. In shops, it's cheaper than a bottle of water. When that's the case, getting drunk makes financial sense.

It's not only beer that Czechs love. The country is one of the most liberal in Europe when it comes to drugs. Getting caught with small amounts is insufficient to be arrested, and only results in a fine equal to a parking ticket. The amounts aren't even that small: fifteen grams of weed, four ecstasy pills, one gram of coke. A 2012 report by Bloomberg crowned the country the "Vice Capital of the World". Assessing various vices - drugs, alcohol, tobacco, and gambling - on a per capita basis, the Czech Republic came top - or perhaps that should be bottom. It's Disneyland for adults, with beer, drugs, and stags wearing fancy dress in place of coke, candy floss, and costumed characters.

GERMANY

BERLIN

Because it's the weekend, because the Berlin Music Festival is happening and, primarily, because of my lackadaisical approach to planning, finding a room is like when Mary had to find one on Christmas Eve: difficult. I'm about to give up and search for a stable, or a park bench at least, when I find the Art Hostel Berlin. Jorg, the owner, who's as bent as a twenty-three euro note, says they only opened five days ago. He shows me to a room and says I'm the first ever person to stay in it. Some aspects of it aren't like a typical hostel room. There's a mannequin in the corner wearing a leather gimp outfit, and spread across the table are gay magazines and flyers for gay bars. And there's a sign on the door: "Gay Boy Room". Pointing at my bed and winking, Jorg says, "The first dream had in a new bed comes true, so make sure you have a good one." I doubt I'll be dreaming tonight. I'll be too scared to sleep.

I shouldn't be surprised. I'm staying in Friedrichshain, the most progressive, multicultural neighbourhood in Germany's most progressive, multicultural city. Berlin has a reputation for welcoming alternative-types and LGBTs from elsewhere in Germany and the rest of the world. It's perhaps something to do with Berlin having to deal with two freedom restricting ideologies - fascism and communism - in the past half-century. Now Berliners say, "Fuck it. Do whatever you want." No one here would think I'm a weirdo for wearing flip-flops in the snow.

Before the Second World War, Friedrichshain was a posh area; now it's rundown, but in a cool way. Dilapidated buildings have been converted into arty pubs and edgy clubs. Apartment blocks have their entire fronts graffitied, and banners promoting peace and love hung from their windows. Every other wall is used as a canvas for artwork; every other lamp post displays posters for weekend parties; every other street corner has a congregation who could be classed as "different" in one way or another. On one corner, three white guys dressed and rapping like black dudes are hooked up to a PA, while skinheads in Doc Martins and punks with blue hair draw on the floor with chalk. Over the rapping, I hear Hitler groaning from the grave.

I stroll beside the Spree River to the longest surviving stretch of the Berlin Wall. At its end in 1989, the concrete section of it ran for 112 km, mostly at a height of three metres. After reunification, Berliners were quick to tear it down, and now only remorseful reminders remain. Some was sold, the rest was dumped. If you want a piece of the wall, I have some for sale for £50 per piece. It doesn't come with a certificate of authenticity, but trust me, it's genuine. Buy three pieces of Berlin Wall and I'll chuck in a piece of moon rock for free. I stand looking at the wall, thinking how terrible it must have been to be stuck on this side of it - the eastern side - being deprived and oppressed by communism. Knowing those on the other side were eating luxury sausages and winning World Cups would have rubbed salt into the wound. Someone who is, say, eighty-five now, and has lived their whole life on the eastern side of Berlin, would have been ten when World War II started, sixteen when Germany lost and Berlin was bombed to rubble, thirty-two when the Berlin Wall went up, and sixty when it came down. That's a hell of a life.

Afterwards, I visit Pankstrasse Station, which those ever-efficient Germans created as a multi-purpose building, functioning as both a metro station and a nuclear bunker. "Beneath Berlin is a labyrinth of thousands of bunkers, shelters, and hideouts," explains Thomas, the tour guide. "They're accessed and connected through secret doorways and passages, that people walk past every day without having any idea they're there." He unlocks a door - an unassuming, unmarked one by a payphone - and we file along a corridor to be confronted by the king of doors: solid metal, half a metre thick, and hydraulically controlled. Beyond it is a decontamination chamber and another door, just as thick and solid. We wander from room to room, through dim-lighted, low-ceiling corridors. The walls are painted pastel green, a colour chosen because it's thought to be the most calming one. Just in case the green isn't enough to take the edge off Armageddon, though, the bunker is suicide-proofed. There are no sharp or glass items, the pipework isn't sturdy enough to hang from, and there are only enough toilet cubicles (which have curtains instead of doors) for each person to spend ninety seconds per day in one. In the sleeping dorms are rows of quad-stacked, super-narrow bunk beds; each with one blanket but no pillow. In the kitchen, there's one bowl per person. Rations would be a single serving of soup per day; partly to make supplies last, partly to stop people blocking the plumbing. Call-out costs for plumbers during a nuclear war are such a rip-off.

"The bunker was built in 1977," says Thomas, "so is quite dated now, but if today there were a nuclear war we could still use it. It's functional and stocked with supplies. It can house 3,339 people for up to two weeks. That's how long the filtered air will last."

How annoyed would you be if you were the 3,340th person in the queue? If you promised to sleep on the floor, eat only toenail clippings, and take just one breath per minute, would they be lenient and let you in? Or, would they leave you outside to melt?

If a nuclear war is to happen, now, while I'm down here, would be a good time. Perhaps I should forget about London and instead stay in Berlin and book myself on this tour every day.

The afternoon is another look at the past as I'm trying to rebuild my cultured persona after drinking my way through Prague. I visit the former headquarters of the Stasi, or Staatssicherheitsdienst, to give them their full name.

Germans are even worse at naming than the Chinese. For forty years the Stasi were the East German equivalent of the Soviet's KGB. Their headquarters have been kept as they were when the building was stormed after the fall of the Berlin Wall. It's a piece of history frozen in time. A mainly brown piece of history. Everything is a shade of brown or so browny a yellow that it may as well just be brown.

Stacks of folders sit on the shelves lining the walls of each room, containing some of the millions of meticulous records kept on one in three East German citizens. The Stasi were tasked with suppressing "subversiveness", a term to which they applied a broad interpretation. People wearing Levi's - a symbol of capitalism - were enemies of the state. If I were here in their heyday, my refusal to wear shoes or trainers would have had me on their watch list - Category A. I'd have been up and over the wall ASAP, and then spent my days flinging dirty protests back over it.

The Stasi wanted to know everything about everyone. The more secrets they knew, the more leverage they had for turning the screw of communism. So they bugged homes, opened private letters, and coerced people into snitching on family and friends. Exhibits show items they used for spying. Cameras and eavesdropping equipment were hidden in everything from briefcases to bird boxes to buttons to books to bras. They wore costumes too; to slyly pass themselves off as postmen, labourers, street cleaners, and the like. I picture a Stasi officer reporting his findings to his superior: "Mr Mielke, having disguised myself as a lamp in the suspect's kitchen for the past fortnight, I can confirm that he has not one but two sausages for breakfast.

Also, I heard him calling you a finger-licking, glory-hole pirate."

One of the rooms displays confiscated items, like music and clothes; and propaganda, like posters and school textbooks. An excerpt from one book says, "Communism is the great creation of society. No normal person can imagine that they can live outside the collective and be happy." Brainwashing children with communism is despicable. I shake my head in disbelief; then I think, actually, we do the same thing now with capitalism, telling kids that no one can be happy without a fast car, large house, luxury holidays, and designer clothes. Maybe future generations, who have jettisoned capitalism in favour of a new 'ism - nudism, satanism, or absurdism - will look back on our, "Me, me, me; buy, buy, buy; work, work, work," brainwashing and shake their heads in disbelief.

Back at the hostel, a Moroccan has moved in. He's sat on the edge of his bed with his head in his hands. "Is this a gay hostel?" he asks when I walk in.

"I think so," I say, pointing at the BDSM gear in the corner and the in-room reading material that contains more willies than words.

"Aww, man; it even says gay boys on the door," he adds, having initially missed the most salient sign that this is a sanctum of sodomy. "It didn't mention this on the website. There's gay-friendly, and there's just gay."

Later, three posh lads join us. If they've been at private school, they'll have had a dabble around the backend. I hope none of them have a dual foot and rubber fetish. My feet in flip-flops will be irresistible.

In the evening, the internet is barely usable. I consider being the wifi Stasi: "Hey you, stop streaming *Will & Grace*. If I catch you at it again, I'll lock you in a wardrobe. And you, with your knob out, turn off that porn. Wait, is that me stripping in a toilet cubicle? I don't know how that got on Pornhub. Have I got many thumbs up?"

NETHERLANDS

AMSTERDAM

I'm staying at Shelter Jordan, a Christian hostel; not to confess and repent my Berlin hostel sins, but because it's affordable and available, which little else is. It's a standard hostel in most respects, but Bible verses cover the walls, and a verbal warning is given at check-in: being drunk or high on the premises gets you kicked out. Reading a couple of chapters of the Bible in a single sitting is their idea of a mad one. I'm sharing a room with two Albanians. One has been living in the US for ten years and sounds like he learnt English solely by watching Al Pacino movies. "These fuckin' Christians," he says, "I never liked 'em, I never trusted 'em. But fuck 'em; I'll be so fuckin' wasted that I won't remember their fuckin' bullshit."

Amsterdam feels more like a town than a city. A painting of a town even. Tall, thin, doll-like houses, with facades more glass than brick, line its sleepy streets and quaint canals. There are so many canals that half the city seems to be water. It has 165 of them, which is more than Venice, championed as the capital of canals. Adding to the sense of being in a centuries-old watercolour is the preference for bicycles over cars. Specifically timeworn bicycles with front baskets and raised handlebars. The Dutch love them more than Alb Fuckin' Pacino hates Christians. The bicycle brigade have commandeered the pavements. The hunted - as cyclists complain they are when they have to cycle on the road - have become the hunters. I propose an Amsterdam Wall, to separate cyclists and pedestrians.

For someone who can't ride a bicycle - me - being here is an emasculating experience. My Mum tells people I never learnt when I was a child because I liked to keep my socks clean. If that's true, I have not only OCD but also amnesia. If that's not true, I'll sue her for slander. Maybe she is telling the truth. It would explain my dedication to flip-flops now - so I can avoid the irksome issue of keeping my socks clean. But why would I care about dirty socks when I don't care about my jeans being dirtier than a dirty old man giving a dirty sanchez to a dirty housewife? To find the truth of the matter, I'll have to buy some socks and get them dirty. If I don't break down in tears, my Mum better hire a bloody lawyer.

I'm joined on the overrun pavements by some people not so prominent in Van Gogh's paintings of Amsterdam: red-eyed stoners, shuffling along seeking munchies. The whiff of weed is widespread, wafting up my nostrils from the many coffee shops in the city. Oddly, the places selling weed are called coffee shops, not weed shops. You can drink coffee at them, but no one does. Thousands are slouched at tables outside them, discussing the themes and theology of *The Empire Strikes Back*.

Scenes of sauciness were also skimmed over by the one-eared wonder in his depictions of Dutch life; which is strange because Amsterdam has no shame about the sex it has on offer. The red-light district is in the city centre, next to Amsterdam's oldest building: a church. It's not just a street but a whole neighbourhood; a nice one with meandering cobblestone streets and picturesque fourteenth-century architecture. Lingerie-wearing women parade their wares in back-lit boudoir windows. Most are attractive, resembling raunchy mannequins, but there are some notable exceptions; like a muscular, pre-op transsexual posturing in bulging panties. Groups of guys linger, wide-eyed and excited - in general, not at Ms Haas De Dyck. They look like teenagers watching the five-minute preview of the porn channel. There's no time wasted going off to a hotel. Knock their door; close the curtains; wham, bam, thank you ma'am; then back on with your day.

Prostitution is legal in the Netherlands, along with all kinds of sex shows, so there's no need for advertising innuendo. Neon lights flash what's on offer:

"No Holes Barred Live Sex."

"Hard Porno Live Show."

"Bondage, Homo, Animal & Teen Sex."

"Special Offer: Tranny Cum Shot."

"Peep Show. 2 Euro/Minute."

As well as sex shows there are sex shops, with all sorts of smut for sale; from dildos in irregular shapes; to portable, plastic fanny tubes; to full-size dolls made of flesh-like material. I make a purchase but can't say what. I want it to be a surprise for my Dad on Christmas Day.

It's not all sex, sex, sex in this area, though; there's also a museum. No, forget that; it's a sex museum.

Returning to the hostel, I stop off to buy magic mushrooms for tomorrow. Half a dozen options are offered, with ratings ranging from "beginner" to "space cowboy". Buying beginner ones would be like ordering a shandy in a pub - out of the question.

I eat half the shrooms for breakfast. With the effects kicking in after thirty minutes, I leave the hostel and walk the streets. Time passes quickly, colours pop and merge, and things far away feel near. When buildings begin to tilt and sway, I take it as a cue to find a bench.

The next hour - or it could be several hours - is like the scene in *American Beauty* where the guy is mesmerised by a video of a plastic bag blowing in the wind: "There's this electricity in the air, you can almost hear it. And this bag was just dancing with me. Like a little kid begging me to play with it. And that's the day I realised that there was this entire life behind things."

My mind wanders to the meaning of life. It is, I decide, "To be yourself, you can't be no one else." It's quite similar to the opening line of *Supersonic* by Oasis, the song I was listening to prior to pondering the meaning of life, but that's probably just a coincidence.

When a woman on a bicycle rides past with a dog sat in the front basket, the thought of her being a chauffeur for VIP dogs keeps me amused for longer than it should. The smirk is wiped from my face by a pigeon that glares at me with evil in its eyes. I stare back at it for ten minutes, at which point it concedes and curtsies.

The giggles return when I realise I'm not morphing into a rainbow, as I temporarily thought I was. It's just my stripy jumper playing tricks on my mind. It's lucky I realised before bending over to create an arc-like shape, which as a rainbow would be logical, but as a man in a stripy jumper would be absurd. People have been sectioned for less.

I look at the remaining shrooms in the bag. Should I? No, but I will. An hour later, I regret eating them. They seem to have shrunk me. I Google "do shrooms make you shrink?" Google says they don't. Next, I Google "Dutch people tall". Google confirms that Dutch people are tall - the tallest in Europe, and the second tallest in the world.

I'm in Dam Square eating a banana, hoping it will soothe my mangled mind, when the Grim Reaper appears, dressed in black and wielding a scythe. First I tell myself it's only a man dressed as the Grim Reaper, then I question whether it's a hallucination. I turn to ask someone but think better of it. "Excuse me, can you see the Grim Reaper?" isn't an appropriate question to ask a stranger. Minutes later, a second Grim Reaper appears; then an alien too.

I'm expecting Jesus next, but instead it's a shirtless, mohawked Australian holding a squash racquet. He holds his arms aloft and squeezes his whole body through the head of the racquet. I've witnessed a miracle. There's no point staying out longer. A dozen plastic bags blowing in a hurricane wouldn't top that. I head back to the hostel, feeling frazzled and needing a nap.

When I wake, I take a train to Hoek Van Holland, a port town in the north-west of the country. I bought a £65 boat ticket to England a few days ago. A speedboat to London would have been the cool option, but coolness costs cash, and I'm skint. Instead I'm travelling by ferry to Harwich, 150 km from the capital.

I sit on a jetty to wait for the ferry, my legs dangling over the side. I take off my flip-flops first, in case they fall off. I'd be gutted not to cross the finish line wearing them. Since Sydney, I've only worn trainers - borrowed ones - a couple of times: on deck on the cargo ship and to play badminton in Bangkok. And my feet have never felt better. I've proven beyond dispute that flip-flops are superior to trainers and shoes. You know what you have to do now: throw your trainers and shoes in the trash; wear only flip-flops.

(Disclaimer: Any reliance placed on the previous statement is strictly at your own risk. In no event will Mark Walters be liable for any loss or damage arising out of it, or in connection with it.)

Late in the evening, the ferry docks. It has lounges, shops, and bars; even a basketball court and cinema. Next time I travel from Sydney to London without flying, I'll take a ship like this the whole way. This time there were occasions I thought I wouldn't make it, but as the ferry departs, it looks like I will. Unless the ferry sinks.

ENGLAND

LONDON

I wake at 6 am and go out on deck to enjoy the view for the homestretch to shore. I'm too late, though; we've already docked. So my first sight of Blighty after nine months away is a busy port, not craggy cliffs and verdant pastures. It's like going downstairs on Christmas morning and finding your parents have bought you Ken instead of Action Man.

I take a train to London, where the trip will end. Having been away for so long, there's a sense of strangeness to being back. Sights and sounds feel surreal; it's as if I'm in a movie. I half-expect Harry Potter and his ginger pal to walk past on their way to Platform 9¾ to embark on another year of trying to get Watson to hold their little pink wands.

After dropping my bag at the hostel, I meet my sister, Kirsty, who's come from Birmingham to meet me. "Mark! I almost didn't recognise you. Where's your beard gone?" she says on seeing me.

"I thought it wise to shave, so MI5 don't think I've been away on a tour of terrorist training facilities."

We catch the Tube to Westminster, where on the banks of the River Thames is the classic scene used by directors to show the action has moved to England: the iconic Big Ben rising beside the grandiose Houses of Parliament, where spectacled, briefcase wankers decide the laws that govern the land. One such law, in the sixteenth century, made it illegal to stand sockless within a hundred metres of the Queen. It's since been repealed, so I don't need to scarper if I see her, to save my feet being spiked on Tower Bridge. Guy Fawkes, a flip-flop wearer peeved at the discrimination, tried to blow up Parliament with fireworks. If he had succeeded, we could have spent the last four hundred years living in a joyful state of anarchy: shagging in the street, eating shrooms for breakfast, and standing sockless within a hundred metres of the Queen.

Across the river, the London Eye, a futuristic Ferris wheel, spins; The Shard, a three-hundred-metre, pyramidal skyscraper, rises; and countless cranes cross the cityscape, adding new layers to new buildings funded by new money from China and Russia. Squares in suits sit sombrely along the riverside, getting forty-five minutes respite from the confinement of their cubicle to eat prawn sandwiches from Waitrose. If I had to spend my days caged in a cubicle, I'd soon be bungee jumping off The Shard - without a bungee cord. Past them saunter designer women with designer dogs in designer bags, and podgy policemen with truncheons and shiny-badged helmets. I've been wary of the police in most of the countries passed through, but British police hold no fear. They're cuddly, not corrupt; more likely to tickle than taser.

Redcurrant telephone boxes and post boxes stand on street corners, like uniformed workers ready to do a day's work, oblivious to the fact that mobile phones and email have left them redundant. And where there's a corner there's also a pub, and at least a couple more between each corner. There are so many pubs because the British love pubs. It could be the social aspect; it could be the terrible weather; or, most likely, it could just be that Brits love getting pissed. It starts with going to the pub for one pint and ends ten pints later. On this point the law-makers got it right: "Thou shalt not leave a pub in the land of England in a state of sobriety. The punishment for non-compliance is to be called a lightweight for a period not less than seven years."

The place for our one pint is Dirty Dicks, a dim-lighted, near-windowless establishment with low timber beams and wood-panelled walls. It's named after a former owner who refused to ever wash again after the death of his fiancé on their wedding day. I'm not quite as dirty as Dirty Dick, but my jeans could do with a good wash. I redirected money for washing detergent to my London Alcohol Reserve. Even in a skanky pub, a pint in London costs £5. Expensive as it is, at least I know I'm paying the same price as everyone else. I'm sure that many times in the past months I've been charged the cost of a Lada for an ice cream.

After drink number six, or maybe nine, in pub number three, or maybe five, Kirsty asks, "When are we going to visit

Big Ben? Last time I came to London, people took the piss because I couldn't find it."

"Are you joking?"

"No. I need a photo of me next to it this time."

"We walked past it this morning. You know, the big clock by the River Thames, next to the Houses of Parliament."

"Was that Big Ben? I thought it was just a big clock."

"Big Ben is a big clock."

We don't make it back to Big Ben, only to more pubs.

As Kirsty's about to set off to get the last train back to Birmingham, I try to persuade her to stay in London: "Book yourself into the hostel I'm at. Don't worry; hostels are fine. Well, the air-con is either too high or too low; there are often stains on the sheets; people piss on the floor; and, wait, actually, hostels are shite. I'd go home if I were you."

For breakfast, I visit a greasy spoon, to eat eggs, bacon, hash browns, fried bread, mushrooms, sausages, and tomatoes; slathered in both brown and red sauce, and washed down with a mug of tea. The best breakfast in the world, for those who don't care about their waistline. Some people - like the French and Italians - look down their nose at British food and say it's unhealthy and tasteless. This irks Brits, especially those who got a Jamie Oliver cookbook for Christmas and so consider themselves a chef. But it's a fair comment. Chips, chops, and pies - the staples of the British menu - aren't the height of culinary sophistication. That Brits half the time eat French, Italian, or Asian food of some variety says, even if they don't admit it, the local options - fried breakfasts aside - aren't all that.

It's not only foreign cuisine that's plentiful but foreigners too: 40% of those living in London were born abroad. A fresh batch of immigrants may soon arrive; this time from Scotland, where a referendum on independence from the UK is taking place in a few days time. The Scots pipe up about independence every time *Braveheart* is aired, and we've said we'll let them vote on it if, in return, they agree to never again show Mel Gibson in a skirt on TV. Newspapers are predicting that the majority of the tartan-wearing Nessie-shaggers will vote for independence. How long will it last, though? Once they've spunked all of their North Sea oil money on whisky and Andy Murray merchandise, they'll ask to rejoin the UK. And we'll have to let them because not to do so is akin to not allowing your retarded brother back in the house after he ran away, £5 note in one hand, knob in the other.

I walk along Jubilee Walkway to Buckingham Palace, past stalls selling slippers, boxers, and mugs emblazoned with the Union Jack. I want to knock the door to let Lizzie know I've made it here from Australia, where she's also the Queen, without flying; but the gilded gates keep me well back. I push my face to the railings and call out, "Queenie, I've brought you some gifts from my travels: some tea from China, a boomerang from Australia, and a Bulgarian from Bulgaria."

She doesn't reply. The guards are no help, stood like statues in fancy dress. Their fluffy bearskin headwear quadruples the size of their head. I'd tell them they look like fat-headed plonkers if I didn't have a strict never-insult-a-man-with-a-gun policy. I adhere to it even when the man with the gun isn't allowed to move.

Leaving the palace, I bump into a man, who apologises to me. You're much more likely to get a "sorry" than a smile from someone in England, where people are frugal with friendliness, profligate with politeness. We'll apologise for everything, regardless of who's fault it is or if an apology is even required. Sorry, but I don't why. Sorry about that. Sorry.

In the afternoon I meet Chris, one of my best mates from uni, at a pub - obviously - for one pint - obviously. We studied for the same degree for four years, and both somehow graduated with a 2:1 despite spending more time playing Pro Evo and popping pills than attending lectures and seminars. Since then, our paths diverged. He knuckled down to London life, while I went gallivanting around the world. Ten years on, he's got more cash than he knows what to do with. "I set up a recruitment company," he says, "and it's done well. I've bought a house in London, and I'm building another in the countryside."

Chris is the exception rather than the rule, though. Most of my peers from uni have slogged for a decade and have little to show for it - perhaps a Ford Focus and a deposit for a one-bedroom apartment in the suburbs. I wouldn't swap my last ten years for that. Those years - twenty to thirty - are a chunk of your peak ones. Money can't buy back those years. But, I guess, only when we're looking back from our rocking chairs when we're eighty will we know which was the right route to take. I hope I'll be able to afford a rocking chair and won't be sitting on the floor.

Afterwards, I head to Trafalgar Square, which marks the centre of London and the end of the trip. Before stepping onto the square, I stop and close my eyes to imagine thousands of people cheering and chanting my name. When I open them, I'm back on the thirty-five-hour bus to Perth. Since then, it's all been a dream. I'm kidding. You haven't spent hours reading fictitious nonsense. It might be nonsense, but it's true.

Nelson's Column stands in the centre of the square. At base of the granite pillar are four bronze lions. I climb on one to sit and think about the trip. I lost track of how much I spent, but estimate it was £7,500-£10,000. I'd have spent an equal amount had I stayed in the UK for the time I've been away. It's been money well spent. Spending on enriching experiences makes more sense than spending on anything else, and the experiences on this journey have improved me, made me stronger and wiser.

I put myself in the hands of the world and wasn't chewed up and spat out. Many more wanted to help than wanted to harm. If I'd listened to the scaremongers, I'd never have started out. They told me the world is fraught with danger, that I'd get attacked, robbed, injured, or sick. But I didn't. To live in fear, is to fear life. I've never felt more fearless. I've never felt more alive.

THE END

To view photos from the trip, visit:
https://www.facebook.com/marktries

ALSO BY MARK WALTERS

India(ish)

Buttock-bruising buses and chock-a-block trains take Mark on a farcical journey around India. Along the way, he sees the awful, the absurd, and the awesome. He travels over Himalayan mountains, across Rajasthani deserts, and through Keralan rainforests; via super cities like Mumbai and Delhi, sacred sites like Rishikesh and Varanasi, and scenic spots like Palolem and Hampi. He encounters randy perverts, mystical madmen, and armed mustachios. He witnesses the barbecuing of bodies beside the Ganges, and Indian and Pakistani soldiers facing off in a Run DMC showdown. He experiences temporary insanity after consuming bhang, and testicular torment doing yoga in skinny jeans. And it all begins with an ill-fated venture to walk across India...in flip-flops.

ABOUT THE AUTHOR

Mark Walters is a travel writer from the UK. He's written a couple of books about his travels, which might be the best travel books ever written. If not the best, probably not the worst.

www.marktries.com
mark@marktries.com

26726598R00109

Printed in Great Britain
by Amazon